P9-DDW-221

MULTICULTURAL MINISTRY HANDBOOK

Connecting Creatively to a Diverse World

EDITED BY

David A. Anderson
& Margarita R. Cabellon

IVP Books

An imprint of InterVarsity Press
Downers Grove, Illinois

InterVarsity Press
P.O. Box 1400, Downers Grove, IL 60515-1426
World Wide Web: www.ivpress.com
E-mail: email@ivpress.com

InterVarsity Press® is the book-publishing division of InterVarsity Christian Fellowship/USA®, a movement of students and faculty active on campus at hundreds of universities, colleges and schools of nursing in the United States of America, and a member movement of the International Fellowship of Evangelical Students. For information about local and regional activities, write Public Relations Dept., InterVarsity Christian Fellowship/USA, 6400 Schroeder Rd., P.O. Box 7895, Madison, WI 53707-7895, or visit the IVCF website at <www.intervarsity.org>.

Design: Cindy Kiple
Images: Qweek/iStockphoto

ISBN 978-0-8308-3844-8

Printed in the United States of America ∞

Library of Congress Cataloging-in-Publication Data

Multicultural ministry handbook: connecting creatively to a diverse world/edited by David A. Anderson and Margarita R. Cabellon.
p. cm.
Includes bibliographical references.
ISBN 978-0-8308-3844-8 (pbk.: alk. paper)
1. Church work with minorities—United States. 2. Race relations—Religious aspects—Christianity. 3. Multiculturalism—Religious aspects—Christianity. 4. Bridgeway Community Church (Columbia, Md.) I. Anderson, David A., 1966- II. Cabellon, Margarita R.
BV4468.M86 2010
253—dc22

2010014319

P	19	18	17	16	15	14	13	12	11	10	9	8	7	6	5	4	3	2	1
Y	26	25	24	23	22	21	20	19	18	17	16	15	14	13	12	11	10		

CONTENTS

123 337

THE BUILDING BLOCKS OF A
MULTICULTURAL MINISTRY

David A. Anderson

IT WAS JUST SHY OF TWENTY YEARS AGO when I, along with a small team of people, parachuted in with flares to Columbia, Maryland, to start an intentionally multicultural, nondenominational, contemporary style, performing arts church that would cause people to long to return to church the next week. We have come very close to such a dream. We are far from perfect, and we have had our challenges along the way, which you will read about throughout this handbook, but the dream is very real and many of us count it a privilege to be a part of it.

If you were to walk into Bridgeway Community Church today, you would feel the presence of God manifested throughout the church. Not in an eerie kind of way, but in a very real and joyful way.

You would be in awe as you scanned the congregation, wondering if the chocolate black faces you saw in the foyer were African Americans from Washington, D.C., or Africans from Lagos, Nigeria, or Nairobi, Kenya. You would wonder if the caramel brown Hispanics were from Mexico, Puerto Rico or the

Bronx. You might look twice at some of the Asians, attempting to figure out if they are Korean or Chinese. After a warm greeting from a smiling Asian woman in the lobby, you would come to realize through conversation that she is neither Korean nor Chinese, but a second generation Filipina who considers this church a family and not simply a group of distant acquaintances who share the same faith. This woman's name is Margarita Cabellon. You will meet her later as one of the contributors to this book and coeditor with me.

"Welcome to Bridgeway" is a common greeting you will hear from the white and black men holding the doors open for you as you enter the building, and from the greeters who will usher you to your seat. It is very possible that you might be the recipient of a warm smile from Lethia, an eighty-something black woman who is sure to remind you that she has more energy than most young people. Kelly, a forty-something white woman, may hand you the morning flyer with an infectious look that warns, "You have no idea what God is going to do in the service you are soon to experience."

While I am at it, allow me to introduce myself to you because you may bump into me on your way into the auditorium where worship services are held. I'm David Anderson, the founding pastor of this crazy place called Bridgeway. I enjoy standing in the lobby and greeting folks as they walk in. I'm an African American male who stands at 6' 3" and delights in high fives, fist bumps, hand shakes, and one-armed bear hugs as I clutch my Bible in my other hand. I'm not easy to get around, so you might feel compelled to smile and greet me on your way in. If by chance you miss me, you might catch Pastor Dave Michener's gracious smile and firm handshake as he uses his left foot as a door stopper, holding it open for you to pass. Dave, who we all call Mich, is the executive pastor, who happens to be a white man with red hair. I assure you that red hair was not on our affirmative action recruiting list, yet our congregation enjoys its abundant share of reds. Some natural, some not. Some we will never know.

Whether you bump into me, Mich, Margarita, Lethia or Kelly, I am confident you will feel a sense of God's presence beginning to shift your mind from the preoccupations of your busy morning to the loving dynamic that so obviously bubbles up through the diverse gathering of this Spirit-anointed body at Bridgeway. The transition begins somewhere between the first wave you receive in the parking lot or the first greeting at the front doors, to the buzz in the lobby or the welcoming words of one of our Spirit-directed worship leaders.

Emnet, a young Ethiopian woman, sits behind the Welcome Desk to greet worshipers. It is possible that she will point young families with children toward our BridgeKids ministry, where the little ones can learn about Jesus in fun, interactive ways. If you're not greeted by Emnet, two white gentlemen sporting ties, Peter or Don, will greet you with a big smile and sincere handshake or a pat on your left arm, inviting you in through our wide glass double doors.

Then there's Jim, an African American male from Philadelphia who moved to Columbia to join Bridgeway as a minister. He's often found floating in the lobby to minister to those in need. If for some reason you miss Jim, you surely won't miss Joseph, a Korean brother with a lively laugh, who is one of our contagious ministers. He will most certainly be staked out near Henry, a black brother full of the Holy Spirit, at our Missions Café. Our café is a place to purchase a cup of coffee, hot chocolate, a muffin or piece of fruit, knowing that every dollar of profit contributes to missions locally and around the world. The café team will not only serve you something to eat or drink but they will minister to your spirit as well. Henry, Joseph and the entire Missions Café team will greet, pray with and encourage you on your way into or out of the weekend services. A part of their routine encouragement is to introduce people to our Life Groups ministry, which is strategically staked out in the middle of the lobby. Life Groups are co-led by Chad, the offspring of a Native American mother and an African American father, and Chris, a white brother who I had the privilege of marrying to a woman who has a Jewish father and a black Hispanic mother. Talk about diversity!

Just like you, each of these people has their own story. No doubt they came to or through Bridgeway because of God's timing and plan for their lives, but still, how is it that they are all here?

How is it that an Ethiopian woman, a racially mixed Native American man, a black-Hispanic-Jewish woman married to a white man, a Filipina woman, a Caucasian woman in her forties, an African American woman in her eighties, a Korean man, and white and black men can all consider Bridgeway Community Church their church home? And why will you encounter these wonderful people before you make it into the sanctuary for worship?

The answer at Bridgeway is clear. Without an intentional vision to start and sustain a church culture that welcomes, accepts, respects and values people from various colors, classes, and cultures, the natural environment—racial exclusivity—would not be conducive to the burgeoning of multicultures. The only way that my executive assistant, a white woman who grew up in Scotland with a Presbyterian background, could find joy and solace for herself and her beautiful redheaded daughter (along with the other reds I have already mentioned) in a place like Bridgeway is because four building blocks of a multicultural ministry were in place: (1) personal calling and commitment of the leader to multicultural ministry, (2) clear vision and staffing for multicultural ministry, (3) intentional pursuit of multicultural ministry and racial reconciliation, and (4) a unified philosophy of multicultural ministry.

BUILDING BLOCK 1: PERSONAL CALLING AND COMMITMENT TO MULTICULTURAL MINISTRY

Every leader has a story. Whether male or female, those who are in ministry have their own God story and, I would suspect, their own race story. In order for a multicultural church to have the drive, the values and even the stomach to make tough choices, the leader has to be called and committed deep within to multicultural ministry.

When I was eighteen years old, I surrendered my stubborn will to the lordship of Jesus Christ. I pulled my car over to the side of the road in Prince George's County, Maryland, where I wept like a baby as I invited Jesus into my life. The Holy Spirit overwhelmed me and captured my full attention as I cried out, "Lord, I'm yours!" After a series of events in my life months prior, under conviction of my sinful ways I finally gave in to Christ on that Sunday afternoon while driving home from church. I asked Jesus to forgive me and save me.

During that time of conviction on the side of the road, I sensed a new direction for my life that was so much different than my aimless pleasure seeking and double-minded living. I wanted to reach as many people for Christ as I could from the moment of my conversion. This compelling desire led me toward becoming a pastor. I began to plan how I could be educated for the task. At the same time, I was envisioning the kind of ministry I wanted. Having grown up in the traditional black church, but living in the racially mixed suburbs of Washington, D.C., I was vexed with a new vision that was undeniable. It was a calling, a compulsion, a "must" in my mind.

I wanted, no, I needed to pastor a church that was racially mixed so all people could come. While I had not seen this kind of ministry before, I could not imagine pastoring only one kind of people, even if they were "my own people." I am sure that my upbringing and a series of unfortunate racial events as a youngster played into my passion to build bridges of reconciliation. (See the books *Letters Across the Divide* and *Multicultural Ministry* for my race stories.) Intuitively I knew my gifts were so much broader and my heart so much bigger than a ministry to a specific people group. For some reason I felt like unicultural ministry would be too confining for me, and I had a deep aversion to limiting my ministry to one race of people.

To this day I still find great comfort in the traditional black church, and it truly feels like the house I grew up in—familiar and foundational. But now I was being called out of the nest, maybe for good.

As I went to Montgomery Community College in town and then transferred to Moody Bible Institute in Chicago, I painted the picture to everyone I knew about what a racially integrated church could and should be. I often received smiles and well-wishes that had the background noise of "That's nice, young man. Good luck," with the subtext, "It will never work." While in Chicago, I served as an assistant pastor for a few years in the poor projects of Cabrini Green, a notorious low-income housing project that was all black at the time. After graduating from Moody, I served as a pastoral intern at a predominantly white church in a Chicago suburb that was affluent and completely opposite of the "projects." Both environments were racially exclusive back then. Yet, I still continued to paint my ideal picture with speeches, conversations and presentations everywhere I went to anyone who would listen.

Starting a racially mixed church was *in* me, and I was prepared to die trying. I was committed to bringing this vision to pass regardless of the scores of professional voices that warned me of failure because of the sociological and homogeneous principles that had defined church planting for generations past.

WHAT ABOUT YOU?

What is your racial story?

When did you know that you were racially different?

Have you ever envisioned a church that was beyond a single race of people?

Is there a people group you have received pain from or you just don't like?

Are you currently in a predominantly single-race church by design or by default?

Why did you pick up the *Multicultural Ministry Handbook?*

PRACTICAL APPLICATION

Write a paragraph defining what you think your church would be like if it were multicultural.

BUILDING BLOCK 2: CLEAR VISION AND STAFFING FOR MULTICULTURAL MINISTRY

My wife, Amber, is a mixed-race Korean and Irish woman who I'm sure married me by faith. What an adventure it would be. She had no idea. Neither of us did, really. I would often tell her during our courtship at Moody about my desires for planting a multicultural ministry. Her school major was in American Intercultural Ministries, so we were thankful there was some synergy. She was always supportive of the vision, but, having grown up in Korea and then being adopted as a teenager by a Caucasian family in a racially segregated America, she too was buying into nothing more than a well-worded ideal. Yet, her faith in God was strong. Her faith in me has always been risky. I am so glad that she took a risk with me, because Bridgeway would not exist today without Amber's wisdom, support and sacrifice. She would agree that it has been a dream most of the time, a nightmare some of the time, but definitely an adventure all of the time! She was my first team member and eventually my first church member. The two of us together were the initial making of a multicultural church.

When I began painting the picture of a multicultural church to college mates, church friends, family members and even strangers, it was clear that I would have to recruit some white folks to start the church with me. I was on the hunt for whites who had the same vision. Thankfully, I found Rich Becker, a white, single, college-age man who was dating a white woman named Beth. They met at the singles group I was pastoring as an intern in the suburbs of Chicago—Willow Creek Community Church.

I promised Rich and Beth three things if they joined me. I promised them that starting Bridgeway would be fun, fulfilling and frustrating. They soon married, and without pay they moved from

Chicago with Amber and me. I have more than delivered on all three promises! To this day, Rich is the executive director of the creative arts at Bridgeway, and Beth is a worship leader and actor.

Locally, I met an African American brother, Chance Michael Glenn, who was a vocalist. We met on a basketball court playing pickup games. I heard Chance humming a familiar Christian tune and from there the friendship began. Only God would know that he would be our first worship leader, setting the course of multicultural worship and praise at Bridgeway. Chance was married to Marsha, a Bahamian woman. She added a touch of the Islands to our mix.

I also received a phone call from a white keyboardist, Brian Johnson, who ran the music department at the local college and was interested in our church plant. They all bought into the vision. Chance led the worship while Brian led the band with some of his college students, including a Filipino drummer and a Filipino bassist. Brian brought on a white lead guitarist named Phil, who often sported a ponytail while making his guitar scream. Brian, his wife Eileen, the Glenns, Beckers and Andersons were a team of early developers who planted a multicultural seed that would one day spring into a harvest for generations to come.

To have a racially mixed core team from the beginning couldn't have made me happier. With the exception of Chance, his wife Marsha, Amber and me, the group was predominantly white. After a year, the Filipino brothers and others began to stick. This was a good and instructive beginning as more staff would come and go over the years. Each time a leader or staff member left, we were racially challenged as the composition of our leadership shifted. I still view such challenges as a good problem to have, one that many churches do not have the privilege of facing.

Staffing Around the Leader

It is imperative that the leadership team supports the vision of multicultural ministry. They need to know that the leader is completely committed to diversity. The team must know that the strategy employed will be racially and culturally inclusive. While everyone on the team may not be as committed to multicultural ministry as the leader, it is important that they understand the vision clearly and are willing to grow in their racial journey. As the years progress, it is not unusual for the church to add and subtract staff members, whether paid or unpaid. It is imperative that race and culture play a key role in hiring anointed people in order to maintain racial balance and cultural perspectives as the ministry grows.

YOUR TEAM

What is the racial make up of the leadership of your church?

How would your church respond if the next two or three employees or volunteers were of a different racial or ethnic background?

How would a diverse leadership team add to the decision making and strategy of the church?

What are you willing to do to attract and recruit people from different racial backgrounds who could draw in others from that same demographic in your area?

PRACTICAL APPLICATION

List the racial and gender makeup of your ministry leadership team and ask yourself who's missing.

BUILDING BLOCK 3: INTENTIONAL PURSUIT OF MULTICULTURAL MINISTRY AND RACIAL RECONCILIATION

On Sunday mornings people must see others that look like them or they will feel like outsiders. Whether intentionally or unintentionally unicultural, a church communicates nonverbally to other racial groups that they are the visitors and this is not "their" church. The goal, of course, is to make people feel welcome and

---

YOUR STAGING AND STRATEGY

What does your stage or platform look like on Sundays, and how could you shift the players around?

Who in your congregation could read the Scriptures, lead songs, give a greeting, share a testimony, preach a sermon or recite a poem?

What kind of background music is playing when people walk in?

What kind of songs do you sing?

What kinds of stories are told?

What kinds of heroes are elevated?

What you see is what you get! How can your church change what others see?

---

accepted in our churches. In order for this to happen, we must be intentional about it.

Not only should we be friendly toward others, regardless of race, but they should feel a sense of identity. When people identify others like themselves in our church, they know they are not alone and the church is indeed a place for them. Otherwise, we may inadvertently communicate that there is a no place for them.

Hence, we are doggedly and proactively intentional when it comes to diversity. Whether we are placing a white and a black man at the front doors or at posts inside the main auditorium, everything is intentional when it comes to creating and sustaining a multicultural environment. This is true especially of the Bridgeway stage on Sundays.

When our worship teams think about our worship leadership, the placement of blacks, whites, Hispanics, Asians, males, females, young and older are taken into account. When we cast a drama or appoint someone to deliver what we call the "community news," we think about who should participate in light of the others who are preaching or administering communion that day. Our African American worship director, Nikki Lerner, and our creative arts director, Rich Becker, will say more about this later in the book. This is one of the most critical areas when starting, sustaining or transitioning a church toward multicultural diversity.

I am often asked how the Holy Spirit can move when things are so well thought out. It's a good question, but I could ask the same question in reverse. How can the Holy Spirit move among unintentional racial exclusivity? Our goal is to intentionally think of the visitor or worshiper who walks through our front doors. We want that person to see someone like him- or herself. There is no doubt that God's Spirit can move in unicultural churches too, but it must please the Lord tremendously to see his children unified in a multicultural environment. What merit is there when a Chinese family walks into a church only to feel unwelcomed and underrepresented in the body of Christ? If there is a large population of Chinese in my local area and I am not reaching out to them in ministry or relationship, I am missing an opportunity for our church to reflect the image of God. This strategy takes relentless evaluation, restructuring and an ever-increasing amount of flexibility.

BUILDING BLOCK 4: A UNIFIED PHILOSOPHY OF MULTICULTURAL MINISTRY

Some of the biggest hindrances to multicultural ministry are the structures in place that keep churches from being more flexible. An example is the way a worship service is conducted. Intentionality is critically important, but what if a denomination or order of service doesn't take into account various styles of expression?

This is a practical hurdle that may limit a church's ability to attract diverse peoples. Another example is the hiring of candidates. This may be a major problem if the pool from which denominational candidates are drawn is limited in its diversity and rules prohibit hiring outside the denomination.

Our structure. At Bridgeway Community Church we are committed to a philosophy of ministry that has worked for two decades. We have chosen to "major on the majors and minor on the minors." When it comes to doctrines and minor theological positions that have divided churches and denominations for centuries, we steer clear. Beyond the major theological deal breakers, we give grace and space for various beliefs. We find that such openness invites diversity and promotes inclusion. What are the deal breakers, you may ask?

Our nonnegotiables, or "deal breakers," are:

1. The triune God is one God in three persons as God the Father, Son and Holy Spirit.

2. Humankind is sinful and needs a Savior. Jesus Christ is that Savior who came to earth and lived a perfect life. He was cruci-

fied, buried and rose again from the dead; Jesus is the only way to God the Father, who offers salvation to all.

3. The church is God's family and the primary agency on the earth to carry the message of reconciliation and communicate God's love to a dying world. The church is empowered by the Holy Spirit to live out the Great Commission that Jesus Christ assigned to his church.

4. Jesus Christ is returning again one day for all who are his, will exact final judgment and will take his followers into eternity in heaven.

Outside of these major theological points, everything else is minor, flexible or a matter of conscience. Individually, we pastors have very strong beliefs based on our culture, upbringing, understanding of Scripture, education and political views. However, we have chosen not to allow these matters to become divisive. Those in our church who have sought to major on minor issues have not found Bridgeway a comfortable fit.

However, the reverse is also true. Because we refuse to divide over doctrine that is not central to redemption, we attract charismatics, Catholics, Baptists, Methodists, Presbyterians, Jews, Arabs, Democrats and Republicans. And even non-Ravens and non-Redskins football fans! This inclusivity has opened the door of discovery for people from different theological backgrounds. They realize that much of their theology was fused with their culture or family upbringing more than with Scripture. Many who have partnered with our multicultural church did not realize how racialized their understanding of doctrine was until they investigated their beliefs more fully. Convictions regarding morality, money, marriage, alcohol, abortion, homeschooling and the like are still important. We have simply chosen not to divide over them.

At Bridgeway these topics are ongoing conversations, not static discussions. We continually talk about the value of our diversity and how it is affected by our dress codes, length of service, level of participation in a service, volume of music, style of prayer and the like. Dialogue must remain open so that sensitivity to the Holy Spirit's movement is a reality and not just a declaration of words.

YOUR STRUCTURE

What theological sticking points would you or your church be willing to flex on if it meant a greater influx of other people groups?

Would you be willing to change your style or length of worship, or method of prayer if it would attract a different demographic?

How difficult would it be to transition toward a more flexible structure, and what would it cost?

How comfortable would your leadership be entertaining such ideas?

We have discussed the four building blocks for multicultural ministry behind the scenes at Bridgeway Community Church. These building blocks are (1) personal calling and commitment to multicultural ministry, (2) clear vision and staffing for multicultural ministry, (3) intentional pursuit of multicultural ministry and racial reconciliation, and (4) a unified philosophy of multicultural ministry.

As you continue reading, I pray that the practicality of these building blocks are peppered through the different voices and expressions of our leadership team. Every church is different. Every ministry is different. God has not called all churches to be alike. However, these building blocks are transferable, and any church can increase its diversity tenfold by intentionally building on the same or similar principles and removing many of the hindrances that keep people away.

2

RELATIONAL TRAINING FOR
A MULTICULTURAL CHURCH

Frank V. Eastham Jr.

So you or your church leadership has decided to move toward multicultural ministry. How do you move toward making your vision reality? You must begin by creating a mindset of multicultural living. David Anderson says multicolored does not mean multicultural. Creating a multicultural ministry requires changing the way we think about living and ministering in our church, neighborhood and workplace with people who come from classes and cultures different from our own. Anderson often reminds us that racism is not a *skin* problem; it's a *sin* problem.

Multicultural living isn't a mere social phenomenon or a social activist movement created by politically liberal individuals. Living life with a multicultural perspective is God ordained. God calls us to be one body, bearing with one another, and being reconciled with one another just as Christ reconciled us with our eternal Father.

This isn't an easy process and is uncomfortable for even the most open-minded, obedient and mature follower of Christ.

Those who provide training in multicultural living must skillfully maneuver participants through conversations that lead to enlightened, honest comprehension. We must help participants become intentional in actions that move them toward multicultural ministry, reconciling people from all cultures and classes.

THE CONTINUUM

Before we can begin to train others in diversity and crosscultural relationships, we need a clear understanding of our own journey and where we are on the reconciliation continuum. It is good to explore the events and interactions in our personal history that have shaped the assumptions we make and the biases we have about others. Unless we take the time to examine our experiences through the multicultural lens that God provides, we may be unaware of our biases.

I grew up attending church, going to school and living in a mono-ethnic community. Although my family would deny being racists, I was taught directly and indirectly that whites are superior to other races and ethnic groups. The whiter the better. My family and community frequently used language that denigrated and demeaned ethnic people groups: Italians, Asians, Hispanics and most definitely Africans and African Americans.

In my twelve years of public education, I remember seeing only two students of color. Unfortunately, I witnessed one of them being beaten in a school stairwell while being instructed that "this is *our* school." I shamefully recall driving through sections of a nearby city where many African Americans lived and yelling racial slurs for Friday night entertainment. I amused my friends, family, teachers and pastors with racial and ethnic jokes and stories. Racism, hatred and cultural division were natural components of my life.

It wasn't until I went on a weeklong Youth for Christ retreat and developed a friendship with two African American students that I realized something was wrong with the way I was living. After a tremendous week of fellowship, learning and a long bus trip home, I hugged and said goodbye to my newfound friends—not knowing if I would ever see them again. When I got to my mother's car across the parking lot, instead of welcoming me home and asking about my trip, the first words out of her mouth were, "Why were you hugging on those n——s?" For the first time in my life, I realized that the n-word was wrong. I vividly remember staring at the dashboard of my mother's car, thinking to myself, *I've got to get out of here.*

Today, I live in Columbia, Maryland—a city designed to connect people from all cultures, classes and religions. I am the principal of one of the most diverse schools in our school district. The school is located in the community in which I live. I also teach culture and diversity classes for a private liberal arts college and was recently appointed by our county executive to sit as a commissioner on the Human Rights Commission of Howard County, Maryland. Over the last sixteen years at Bridgeway Community Church, one of the few multicultural megachurches in the nation, I have become a lead teacher of diversity and relational training and the co-leader of our missions ministry. My work with the missions ministry has taken me to Kenya four times, one of the purposes being to assist Kenyan community leaders with cross-tribal relationship-building training. I sometimes have to pinch myself to make sure I'm not dreaming.

Not everyone has such a dramatic conversion. However, a key component of reconciliation training is to help each person in the body of Christ explore his or her unique cultural journey and make a decision to move toward becoming a racial reconciler.

In *Multicultural Ministry: Finding Your Church's Unique Rhythm*, David Anderson presents a continuum of reconciliation that parallels the continuum of faith found in evangelism (see fig. 2.1).[1] One of the first homework assignments for participants in my reconciliation-training seminars is identifying where they are and where they believe our church is on the continuum. At our next class we discuss our answers. It is important for everyone to see they are in different places and that they will be accepted by others regardless of where they are on the continuum. This exercise also provides good feedback to the church leadership team regarding where people believe the church is on the continuum and creates a sense of urgency in the pursuit of a racially reconciled church.

Intentionality is a theme heard throughout this book and is a foundational principle of our church. We believe that intentionally seeking to be a reconciler and building crosscultural relationships is one of the many disciplines God has called us to practice.

Just as we are at different places on the continuum of faith, we all enter the continuum of racial reconciliation at different points. When training members of our church, we do not want them to feel judged by their point of entry onto the continuum. The continuum allows us to help folks realize where they are and where God wants them to be. It also assists us in conveying the realization that racial reconciliation is a process, not an event. I'm always a little wary of people who place themselves at the end of the continuum. Participants in our training sessions need to be aware of the stages they will pass through on their way to becoming a rec-

---

[1]See David A. Anderson, *Multicultural Ministry: Finding Your Church's Unique Rhythm* (Grand Rapids: Zondervan, 2004), pp. 97-101.

Racist–cynic–agnostic–seeker–**Conversion**–babe–child–teen–adult–**Reconciler**

The **racist** is one who harbors ill feelings, and possibly hatred, toward a particular person or group of people because of color, class or culture. These feelings cause such people to speak, act or think negatively toward other groups.

The **cynic** doesn't really care about other races or racial issues and is happy being with his or her own kind.

The **agnostic** is a pessimist about any change ever truly happening regarding racial issues and is unwilling to seek out change or make concerted efforts.

The **seeker** is somewhat ignorant about racial issues but is willing to learn and has a desire to grow in this area.

Conversion is the point where people realize that God wants them to deal with racial issues in their own heart and in society. They have awakened to the knowledge that things are desperately wrong in the area of race relations in themselves and in the world. They have realized that God desires them to make a difference in this area personally and in society.

The **babe** is newly born in awareness of racial issues and of the need to deal with issues of race in order to be all that God has called them to be. They are dependent on others to help feed and lead them regarding this new area.

A **child** is a young and growing learner who is active in ascertaining information regarding race while trying to apply new knowledge.

A **teen** is a developing and maturing grower in the area of reconciliation. The teen applies reconciliation principles while periodically failing in doing so. They both win and lose as they struggle through reconciliation issues and relationships.

The **adult** is active in taking responsibility as a reconciler and contributes where he or she can to make reconciliation happen. The adult is a bridge-builder who is still growing and learning, yet is far enough ahead in the area of reconciliation to help others grow along the continuum.

The **reconciler** is fully devoted to being a change agent, and understands that God has called him or her to be an ambassador of reconciliation. These people seek education on topics related to race relations and are developing crosscultural relationships with those of other races. They seek to be channels of God's love, grace, justice and forgiveness through friendships and societal contributions.

Figure 2.1. Racial reconciliation continuum

onciler. We can never check reconciliation off our to-do list. Reconciliation is a continuous process of growth and development.

It is important for trainers to share their journey. Being a Christ-follower does not automatically mean we are reconcilers. Participants in our training sessions need to hear firsthand how we can develop the discipline of reconciliation.

Though I became a Christian at age twelve and was a firm follower of Christ for many years, I was caught up in the sin of racism and cultural hatred. Participants must realize that becoming a church member doesn't make us reconcilers. Martin Luther King Jr. once said that eleven o'clock on Sunday morning is the most segregated hour in America.

People who have not participated in direct acts of racism are often confused about why it is important for them to engage in the ministry of reconciliation. They believe their lack of negative experiences qualifies them for being a racially reconciled person. They gain insight into this when they regularly interact with people across cultures. Doing life in a crosscultural manner is the goal.

THE CALLING

I plan training sessions with the realization that the participants will be at various points on the continuum. It is my job to equip them to move forward, either toward the point of conversion or from the point of conversion toward becoming a reconciler. It is important for participants to understand that Christians are called to be one body and to unite with one another. God commands Christians to live a life of multicultural ministry.

The key Scriptures I use as a basis for multicultural ministry are

• Colossians 3:1-14—conversion: turning away from the world

- 2 Corinthians 5:16-21—reconciling with Christ
- 1 Corinthians 12:12-26—reconciling within the church
- Ephesians 4:1-4—reconciling with others

Conversion: Turning Away from the World

If we are to fully understand the calling that God has for multicultural ministry, we must first understand that we cannot simultaneously serve the world and Christ. We must turn away from the world and the beliefs the world has about people. We must understand that in Christ reconciliation occurred between God the Father and humans. God sacrificed his Son in order to reconcile the world to himself. His son, Jesus Christ, represents the world in the sense that Christ entered the world as fully human and fully God. However, in order for the world to be able to live with God for eternity, the human side of Christ had to be sacrificed so that reconciliation could occur.

The same is true for us. If we are to be reconcilers, we must sacrifice our worldly views. We can no longer have the world's view of the people God created. God says,

> Put to death . . . whatever belongs to your earthly nature. (Colossians 3:5)

> But now you must rid yourselves of all such things as these: anger, rage, malice, slander, and filthy language from your lips. (Colossians 3:8)

Have you ever associated any of these words with racism and ethnic division? Each of these words describes sinful actions that people take against others. God blatantly relates this to crosscultural relationships. We are instructed:

Here there is no Greek or Jew, circumcised or uncircumcised, barbarian, Scythian, slave or free, but Christ is all, and is in all. (Colossians 3:11)

God is clear. If we desire to be part of his kingdom, we must intentionally make a decision to flee the ways of the world and turn toward Christ. On our continuum this is the point of conversion.

Reconciling with Christ

Through Paul, God explains how he modeled through Christ the ministry of reconciliation. The New International Version of the Bible even uses the word *reconciliation*. God calls us, as Christ followers, to be Christ's ambassadors.

Paul instructs us that our love for Christ should "compel" us to live for the one who died for us, not for ourselves. In turning away from the world, we are living examples of the depth of love that God has for us.

From now on we regard no one from a worldly point of view. Though we once regarded Christ in this way, we do so no longer. Therefore, if anyone is in Christ, he is a new creation; the old has gone, the new has come! All this is from God, who reconciled us to himself through Christ and gave us the ministry of reconciliation: that God was reconciling the world to himself in Christ, not counting men's sins against them. And he has committed to us the message of reconciliation. We are therefore Christ's ambassadors, as though God were making his appeal through us. We implore you on Christ's behalf: Be reconciled to God. God made him who had no sin to be sin for us, so that in him we might become the righteousness of God. (2 Corinthians 5:16-21)

Reconciling Within the Church

First Corinthians informs the church of Corinth how they are to relate to one another in the church. Right in the middle of the book, as if it really doesn't even belong, Paul uses the parts of the body to provide a lesson in racial reconciliation.

> The body is a unit, though it is made up of many parts; and though all its parts are many, they form one body. So it is with Christ. For we were all baptized by one Spirit into one body—whether Jews or Greeks, slave or free—and we were all given the one Spirit to drink.
>
> Now the body is not made up of one part but of many. If the foot should say, "Because I am not a hand, I do not belong to the body," it would not for that reason cease to be part of the body. And if the ear should say, "Because I am not an eye, I do not belong to the body," it would not for that reason cease to be part of the body. If the whole body were an eye, where would the sense of hearing be? If the whole body were an ear, where would the sense of smell be? But in fact God has arranged the parts in the body, every one of them, just as he wanted them to be. If they were all one part, where would the body be? As it is, there are many parts, but one body.
>
> The eye cannot say to the hand, "I don't need you!" And the head cannot say to the feet, "I don't need you!" On the contrary, those parts of the body that seem to be weaker are indispensable, and the parts that we think are less honorable we treat with special honor. And the parts that are unpresentable are treated with special modesty, while our presentable parts need no special treatment. But God has combined the members of the body and has given greater

honor to the parts that lacked it, so that there should be no division in the body, but that its parts should have equal concern for each other. If one part suffers, every part suffers with it; if one part is honored, every part rejoices with it. (1 Corinthians 12:12-26)

Paul very clearly communicates to us that no race is more important than another. He instructs us that we "all" are the body of Christ. We must remember that God uses the analogy of a married couple to illustrate the importance of the church and the union the church has with Christ. God calls us the church the "bride" of Christ.

Therefore, we must heed God's call to the ministry of reconciliation. We, as individuals, are not alone in this calling. God has a corporate calling for the church to be a leader in this ministry. Every Christian church in the world should be intentionally and strategically equipping its members for the ministry of reconciliation.

Reconciling with Others

God never asks us to do anything he does not equip us to do. In Ephesians, God gives us some very specific instructions for how to live as reconcilers. He acknowledges that it is not easy and will involve conflict, but he reminds us that it is our calling.

Paul drills down to the essence of what our individual interactions should look like when we are living lives worthy of the sacrifice that God made for us.

Be completely humble and gentle; be patient, bearing with one another in love. Make every effort to keep the unity of the Spirit through the bond of peace. There is one body and one Spirit—just as you were called to one hope when you were called—one Lord, one faith, one baptism; one God and Father of all, who is over all and through all and in all.

But to each one of us grace has been given as Christ apportioned it. (Ephesians 4:2-7)

THE CONVERSATION

The topic of diversity can paralyze us to the point that we are afraid to talk about it. The last we thing we want to do is offend someone in this area. Unfortunately, we can never really comprehend what it means to be a multicultural army of fully devoted followers of Christ unless we have conversations about what this means.

I begin every session with a very simple exercise that I learned from Brenda and Franklin CampbellJones, who facilitate cultural proficiency training sessions throughout the country. I have an assortment of rubber bands in the center of the table and ask each participant to play with a rubber band. I ask them to stretch it. Release it. Double it and stretch it again. I ask them to compare their rubber band with their neighbors'. I have them describe how it feels. Describe how the tension changes as they make it bigger and then make it smaller. Describe how their rubbers bands are different.

I use this exercise and these questions to communicate how this will resemble our training session. We all come to the session in slightly different places. Each of us has been stretched to different lengths. Some of us have more tension around this topic than others. We might be afraid of breaking and hurting someone or ourselves. I use two African proverbs to explain our anticipated speed and distance.

We must go slowly to go far.

and

> If we want to go fast, we go alone; however, if we want to go far, we go together.

I also begin with some rules of engagement that are usually developed together. However, I guide the discussion to make sure the following rules are included:

- Listen and speak with an open mind.
- Take risks.
- Allow people to make mistakes.
- Demonstrate mercy to those who make mistakes.
- Demonstrate respect toward others—even if you don't respect or agree with their opinion.
- Relate with others.
- Leave politics out of our discussion.
- What we say here stays here.

As I move through the training sessions, I begin with low-risk activities and discussions, and then move toward higher risk activities and discussions. Moving too fast will cause people to avoid being vulnerable with one another and will affect the growth that both individuals and the group can experience.

Example of a low-risk activity and discussion questions
Activity
Brainstorm:

- events in the world related to racism

- people related to racism
- behaviors related to racism

Questions

- What were my parents' feelings toward people from different cultures and classes?
- How did the media portray people from different cultures when I was growing up?
- How are people from different cultures portrayed today in the media?
- How did my church portray people from different cultures?

Example of a moderate-risk activity and discussion questions
Activity

Divide participants into pairs. Instruct them to predict the following about their partner without having any type of verbal or nonverbal communication.

1. language(s) spoken

2. cultural heritage

3. hobbies

4. favorite
    - movie type
    - food(s)
    - music

After they make their predictions, have participants check out their accuracy with their partners.

Debrief by asking the following questions:

- How did you feel making the predictions? Why?

- Why was this uncomfortable or difficult?

- Were you mostly accurate? Inaccurate?

- Did you knowingly omit a prediction because you didn't want to take a chance of offending your partner?

Questions

- Who were my five closest friends growing up? Did I have a diverse group of friends?

- What kinds of feelings or perceptions did I have about people who were from different cultures other than my own?

- Who was the first person that I developed a relationship with from a different culture? What were some positive and negative experiences related to this relationship?

- Discuss examples of people who have dealt with racism in a Christlike manner or a worldly manner.

Example of a high-risk activity and discussion questions
Activity

Have participants divide by ethnic groups. Ask them to list stereotypes of other ethnic groups. After each group is finished, have them share their responses with the other groups. After a group shares their stereotypes about a particular group, allow that group to respond to the first group. Continue this until each group has had an opportunity to share their responses and obtain feedback from the other groups.

Debrief by asking the following questions:

- How did this activity challenge you?

- What new learning do you have because of this activity?

- Does this confirm or challenge stereotypes that you have about different ethnic groups? Why?

- Why is it important to identify stereotypes that are made about different ethnic groups?

- How can we use this information to build, maintain or repair crosscultural relationships?

The leader who facilitates these seminars needs to be prepared for tension to occur during the sessions, especially when the activities become more intense and require participants to become increasingly vulnerable. The leader should not consider this a bad thing. It actually means that the participants are letting their guard down and speaking from their hearts. This is a desired outcome. It is important, however, that these situations are managed well.

One of the first things a leader should do in this situation is to acknowledge the tension or possible tension. Let the group and the individual(s) affected know that you are aware that the question asked or the comment made might have caused some uneasy feelings. This will reduce the fear the group might have about your awareness and ability to maintain a safe environment.

Ask some clarifying questions to find out exactly what the participant was trying to communicate or ask. The tone should be information seeking, not judging or condemning. This is an excellent time to remind everyone about the reconciliation continuum and the rubber-band activity, and that we are all at different places on the continuum. Reinforce that it is okay to make mistakes and that the group is responsible to demonstrate mercy.

Once enough information is gained to move forward, the leader will want to address how this comment or question might illicit negative feelings among some people groups and then ask members of the group to confirm or deny your assertion. If there are some participants who agree with your assertion, give them an opportunity to discuss their feelings. Monitor the emotional level of the group and proceed on the basis of your read of the group or individuals. If you need to take a break so you can have private conversations or regroup, do so.

Finally, remind participants that these teachable moments are the fuel for helping people move along the continuum toward reconciliation. Pastor Anderson often reminds us that "comprehension begins with conversation." We want to encourage and support productive conversations, even when they get messy. Reconciliation is not a neatly packaged process. It requires persistence, patience and compassion for all of God's people.

I remember a time during a session when we were having some moderate-risk discussions and a question came up about what we should call people from Asian countries. I took this opportunity to communicate some learning I had gained over the years about how offensive it was to call all Asian people Chinese. In fact, some Korean friends explained that being called Chinese was similar to an African American being called the n-word.

At that very moment a Caucasian woman raised her hand and asked, "May I stop you for a moment so that I can ask my friend sitting next to me for forgiveness?" I agreed. As a group, we all got to watch a tremendous act of reconciliation. She turned to Choi sitting next to her and asked, "Are you from China?" When he responded that he was not from China but from Korea, she immediately extended her hand to him and asked him to forgive her for asking him when he had moved to America from China. She explained that she had no idea how offensive it was to assume that all Asians are from China. He passionately forgave her. They shook hands and a relationship was strengthened.

It is essential for the leader to create an environment that supports participants in asking forbidden questions and making innocent mistakes. When this occurs, the growth of the group and individuals is amazing.

THE CONNECTIONS

Building, maintaining and repairing crosscultural relationships forms the building blocks for effective multicultural ministry. Mastering the skills necessary to connect across cultural lines requires us to manage the assumptions we make about others and others make about us. There are three steps in the process of managing assumptions.

Step 1: *Acknowledge* that everyone makes assumptions.
Step 2: *Analyze* why these assumptions are being made.
Step 3: *Act* out reconciliation.

Acknowledge Assumptions

An important step in equipping people to connect with others across cultural boundaries is helping them understand that everyone makes assumptions about others. Those assumptions are both positive and negative. Unless people acknowledge this, they will not effectively move toward becoming reconcilers. Sin is a fact in this world. We cannot escape it until we are on the other side of glory. Until that moment, I believe that we all are susceptible to making negative assumptions about others.

Additionally, we must examine the assumptions others make about us based on our color, class or culture. Understanding what others think about us helps us manage our behaviors that confirm or challenge these perceptions. We have some responsibility to make sure that negative assumptions are challenged. The mere thought that someone might perceive me as feeling dominant and superior because I am a white male can change the way that I choose to approach him or her. I can make sure my verbal and nonverbal language does not convey and confirm this negative assumption.

Analyze Assumptions

The second step in managing assumptions is to analyze why we have the negative assumptions that we do. We need to look at the experiences that have shaped our views so that we can figure out why we assume the things we do about different people groups.

Often, we make assumptions based on limited or, even worse, no experiences. Growing up in an all-white neighborhood I had absolutely no daily interaction with anyone of color. The only source of knowledge I had was my family members' stories and the media. This limited source of information didn't stop me from making sweeping assumptions about every ethnic group other than my own.

Act Out Reconciliation

Acts of reconciliation require us to look at two sets of histories and make critical decisions based on analysis of these histories. When I hear the word *reconciliation* I think of my checkbook. Each month we sit down, sometimes for hours, trying to make sense of two different sets of records. We check the balance the bank says we have and then try to figure out why our checkbook has a different balance. After analyzing two different histories of activity, we make adjustments to reconcile the records. We don't simply get rid of or ignore one set and accept the other. We use both sets of information to accurately determine how much money we have in our account.

We must engage in a similar process in our approach to racial and ethnic reconciliation. We must look at cultural histories and multiple sets of records that shape our current behavior. We can't assume that one set of records is more accurate than another because one set might have had experiences that the other didn't. Only after conducting this dual analysis can we gain an understanding that will allow us to consistently demonstrate behaviors that lead to reconciled crosscultural relationships.

Reconciliation requires us to *connect* with people across cultures. Being *close* to people from other cultures is not enough. In a world that is increasingly diverse, we can sometimes mislead ourselves to believe that just because we live, shop, attend school or even church with people from different backgrounds, we are ministers of reconciliation. This, however, is not true.

Pastor Anderson illustrates the point with an analogy to explain the importance of being connected, not just close, to God. Most of us are probably familiar with the rechargeable lawn and garden equipment that must be plugged into an outlet between uses. When we finish trimming the lawn we place the trimmer on a cradle or attachment device so its battery is connected to the electrical outlet. If it isn't correctly positioned in the cradle, the connection won't be successful.

Those of us who have owned such equipment have on occasion had the equipment quit working after a couple of seconds of use. We realize that when we last used it, we didn't place it correctly in its cradle. It might have been *close* to correct, but it wasn't *connected*. Therefore the battery didn't get recharged.

A similar connection is required for us to experience crosscultural connection and practice the ministry of reconciliation. Being close to people from diverse backgrounds is not enough; we must connect with them. Just like rechargeable lawn equipment, we cannot assume that being physically close to people from different cultures and backgrounds will allow us to build and maintain reconciled relationships. The fuel for acts of reconciliation comes from acknowledging and analyzing the assumptions we make about others and they make about us, and intentionally connecting with each another on a consistent basis.

SUMMARY

As church leaders we must understand that the ministry of reconciliation bears fruit through strategic planning and intentionality. Multicultural ministry does not come through a multicolored worship team, leadership team or congregation. While each of these is important, the most essential task for a church desiring to create a ministry of reconciliation is to change the mindset of the people within the church.

In order for this to occur we must understand that God calls us individually and corporately to be ministers of reconciliation. Through systematic training sessions we must strive to move church members along the reconciliation continuum toward becoming racial reconcilers. Providing opportunities for individuals to have courageous conversations in a safe and structured environment will help create a culture of crosscultural connectedness. Sustaining these connections will equip our churches to become multicultural armies of fully devoted followers of Christ moving forward in unity and love to reach our community, our world and all cultures for Jesus Christ.

Kelleigh's Story

Kelleigh Johnson is a Caucasian female. She attended a white suburban church for ten years prior to finding Bridgeway. She loved her church, but it bothered her that it did not reflect the racial diversity of the surrounding community. After going on overseas missions trips, Kelleigh realized she needed to be more intentional about developing relationships with people from different ethnic and socioeconomic backgrounds. As the Lord would have it, Kelleigh met three people in the same week who all attended Bridgeway.

"As soon as I walked in, it felt right," Kelleigh said of her first visit to Bridgeway. "There was an authenticity in the way I was greeted and felt welcomed by African American people."

Soon after that first visit, Kelleigh signed up to be a greeter with Bridgeway's Frontline Ministry and attended a racial reconciliation workshop led by Frank Eastham, a teacher in the church. During that workshop she sat next to Tamia, an African American female who has since become one of Kelleigh's closest friends.

As a result, Kelleigh joined a Racial Reconciliation Life Group that went through the book *Letters Across the Divide* by Dr. David Anderson and Brent Zuercher. Kelleigh said it was a truly eye-opening and life-changing experience. She remembers "walking in as a defensive white person" and afterward "walking out as a mercy-giving, understanding person."

When asked what the key to this transformation was,

Kelleigh said you have to "allow Christ to change you and he will provide the opportunities. We try so hard as white people that we overcompensate and come off as insincere." She has also learned that you must "be open and listen. Don't be defensive. Hear people's stories. You think you know what their experience has been, but you don't know."

The biggest change in Kelleigh's life is that she feels she is now a more sensitive person in regards to race. "God has given me a new lens to see the world." And she now has numerous friends she calls brothers and sisters in Christ from a wide array of cultural backgrounds.

3 LESSONS LEARNED BY A WHITE PASTOR IN A MULTICULTURAL CHURCH

Dave Michener

I MET DAVID ANDERSON AND DAN TAYLOR in June 1995. We sat together in a class as a part of our graduate school program. At the time I was a youth pastor living in my hometown in Ohio, exactly 3.1 miles from free childcare (aka grandparents) for my sons. My ministry was going great! I was at the top of my professional game as a youth pastor—led a sizeable youth group, exhibited my craziness and creativity without being called into more than one or two deacon meetings a year for a verbal reprimand, felt appreciated by the students and their parents, and enjoyed working with a volunteer staff of wonderful people I called my friends. I also had an antirecession ministry budget, salary and benefits that would be coveted by other youth pastors of churches twice our size.

In that week-long graduate class on leadership in Chicago, I had the opportunity to hang out with David and Dan. I really liked these guys. David was a young, tall and handsome black man with a vibrant personality. Dan was a short white guy who was working in the marketplace so he could support his family as he served as a leader at Bridgeway. Dan was a brilliant and funny guy. It was obvious from the get-go that these two guys were real-deal friends. This intrigued me. And the passion they shared about their little church of seventy people made me jealous. I wasn't looking for a ministry move, but God had been moving in my heart about multicultural ministry. By the end of that week David asked me to join him in helping fulfill his God-given vision of creating a church that would become "a multicultural army of fully devoted followers of Christ, moving forward in unity and love to reach our community, our culture and our world for Jesus Christ" (Bridgeway's vision statement). So I immediately said yes and left my white world flowing with cash and comfort, and moved to the mission field of Maryland. Not!

Sensing the timing was not right for such a drastic move for my family I said no to joining the Bridgeway team and went home. I worked hard at my church while God worked hard on getting me ready for the Bridgeway adventure. God began to grow the seed of desire for multicultural ministry in my heart. For two-and-a-half years my relationship with David and Dan continued as we took an occasional class together, even rooming together for the week of the class. The thought of being part of such a church never left me.

So, in January of 1998, I packed up my family, all our stuff and moved to Maryland to be a part of a small church with a big mission: "building into one another as we build bridges to our community." There were 175 people there on my first Sunday. There was no salary for my family. No youth ministry budget. No office. And no snow! (I was so grateful to be rescued by God from the heat of eternal hell through salvation *and* from the freezing temperatures of eternal winters in the Cleveland area through relocation.) We followed the call and not the cash, and our lives are so much richer because of it.

Now that I have more than a decade of multicultural ministry experience under my belt, I feel strongly about sharing some of my lessons with you—some of which were learned easily and some not. Here are three foundational lessons I've learned as a white pastor in a multicultural church.

LESSON 1: BEING COMES BEFORE DOING

I had to become a multicultural minister before I could do multicultural ministry. If I said my mom was my anchor while growing up, I would have to say that my dad was the wind in my sails. My father is a great dad. My experiences with him through the years have made me the man I am today—and I mean that in the very best way. Growing up with David L. Michener Sr. made me want to be a dad. And if I could have a similar relationship with my kids that my dad had with me, I would die a happy man. Hence, I developed a passion for fatherhood as a very young man. This fervor for fatherhood showed up in stories, events I planned in our church and in my everyday life with my three sons. Many people have asked me to write a book about fatherhood, but even though I have been passionate about fatherhood from my youth, I have not begun to draft a book. Why? Because I want to fully experience fatherhood before I would write about it. What credibility would a book have if written by someone who wasn't a father?

The same is true of multicultural ministry. You must become a multicultural *minister* in order to do multicultural *ministry*. No short cuts. I've had conversation after conversation with passionate pastors who want to have multicultural ministries but have not become multicultural ministers. Tasks become ministry when they are done with the right motives and are in service to other people. That's right—*people*. Ministry requires interacting with human beings. We might call them "sheep," but they are actually people.

So the first question to ask yourself is: *Do I have relationships (and not just contact) with people of other cultures?*

If not, you really can't have a multicultural *ministry*. You simply have multicultural *ideas*. Ideas are not the same as ministry. Ministry is about people loving other people out of the overflow of love they have received from God. Ideas don't need love; people do.

Before you disqualify yourself for not having names like Tyrone, Dong, Marcos, Tanesha or Atar in your phone's Fave Five, stop for a minute and reflect on your life. Here are some things I've done that have fast-tracked me on the unofficial multicultural-minister-in-training continuum.

Pay attention to your past. Since you are reading a book titled *Multicultural Ministry Handbook*, it's probably safe to say that God has been leading your thinking, feelings and desires to ideas of racial reconciliation, social justice and cultural proficiency. Looking back, you'll probably see that God has set markers for multicultural ministry in your life.

I was always curious how we could sing about the love of God in church on Sunday and be forced to memorize Ephesians 4:32— "Be kind and compassionate to one another . . . "—but it was okay to tell insulting jokes about people of color. This puzzled me as a youth. I saw a double standard when I was not permitted to call my sisters names but was allowed to use racial slurs. Why did we applaud (and pay lots of money for) missionaries who were sharing Christ with people from other countries and cultures, and then think it was perfectly acceptable to make condescending and stereotypical remarks about those same people's family members living in the United States?

In some ways I grew up a Christian racist; however, I began to reject this thinking at a very early age. (By the way, my parents have been such an encouragement to me, as I have witnessed their dramatic movement in their racial unity journey. They are not the same people now as they were back then.) Not only was I bothered by the stinkin' thinkin' of racism in the church, I spoke out against it as a teenager. While doing this I noticed not only a disdain for racism but an attraction to other cultures. I began to appreciate other cultures more fully in college as I shared dorm space with a couple of black brothers from D.C. and became close friends with a Filipino guy who actually took me to the Philippines for a summer. God placed me in a predominately white Christian college (99 percent) yet allowed me the privilege of being connected with the few people of minority cultures that were there. These friendships were instrumental in the sculpting of my multicultural heart.

What about you? What experiences and relationships has God used in the process of making you a multicultural minister? What crosscultural friendships do you currently have that will not only afford you opportunities to learn to be more culturally proficient, but also enrich your life by creating a history that will lead to your future in multicultural ministry?

Press on to be a student of racial reconciliation, multicultural ministry and cultural proficiency. Read books, visit museums with people of other cultures and then discuss not only what you *learned* but what you *felt*. Pay attention during the experience and during the following discussion.

One of the most profound experiences in my life was when I visited the Civil Rights Museum in Memphis with one of my closest black friends. I'll never forget seeing him stare into the eyeholes of the hood worn by a Ku Klux Klan member. We couldn't talk about it at first, but after some time to breathe, he opened his mouth—and his heart. That kind of stuff can't be learned from books.

Participate in a multicultural discussion group on racial reconciliation. You don't have to do something extraordinary to experience something extraordinary. Your continuing education as a student can stem from participating in a racial-reconciliation small group. A great place to start is *Letters Across the Divide* by David Anderson and Brent Zurcher. I was a participant in a group like this, and it was the single most enlightening vehicle used by God to move me from being simply reconciled (a multicultural minister) to someone who is a reconciler (a multicultural ministry). I endured the painful stories of friends of other races who were treated unfairly and in unbiblical ways by people of my race. I learned to listen to understand. It was only when I first understood that I could learn to appreciate all they had been through and the incredible beauty of our reconciled relationships.

LESSON 2: AUTHENTICITY WILL ALWAYS GAIN AN AUDIENCE

I must be myself. When I had my initial conversations with David Anderson about moving my family from my Midwest white world to the multicultural metroplex of the Baltimore-D.C. corridor, I asked him, "How do you know that I'll be accepted as not only a friend but a leader by people of color? What advice can you give me?" David looked me in the eye and flashed his charismatic smile and said, "Mich, just be yourself!" Not a week goes by, even after serving eleven-plus years at Bridgeway, that I don't think about this advice. When I follow it, my ministry flourishes. When I begin to try to squeeze into the mold of another person's idea of what an executive pastor in a church of two-thousand-plus people should look and sound like, my ministry gets stifled. I certainly believe that God appoints and anoints certain leaders at certain times for certain people groups for certain tasks. Ephesians 2:10 says, "For we are God's workmanship, created in Christ Jesus to do good works, which God prepared *in advance* for us to do" (emphasis added). My God-designed uniqueness has been created by God to do some God-designed unique things. I need to humbly yet boldly lean into the calling and the authority that God has bestowed to me.

For the longest time my personal mission statement was "I want to live, love and lead like Jesus." It stopped right there. It meant it. The statement summed up my motivation for living and was my definition of success. It was simple enough for a fourth grader to understand. And most important, it could fit on a T-shirt. But over time, I realized it was missing something—*me*. I am crazy enough to believe that God created me, yes, *me*, on purpose. And therefore I *have* a purpose based on my God-designed uniqueness. I can't accomplish that purpose if I'm attempting to be anything other than who God made me to be. Not only was I positionally set apart for personal relationship with God when I crossed the line from unbelief to belief in Christ, but moment by moment I am being progressively set apart, molded and morphed to be more like Jesus as I lean into obedience in responding to the circumstances God allows in my life and learn to practice the great expectations that God has for me (Romans 8:28-29).

So, by the power invested in me by, well, *me*, I have amended my personal life's mission statement to say, "By God's grace, I will live, love and lead like Jesus *while being the best version of myself.*" So help me, God!

Trying to be someone else does damage not only to the kingdom of God but to yourself. After all, God designed the kingdom strategy with *you* in mind. If *you* aren't being *you*, then who is? Living your life as a poser, a clone, a plastic leader creates duplicity of heart. This can cause a person to distrust others and God, shrink back when smothered with stress, and doubt when making dangerous decisions. It's downright unhealthy and can lead to discouragement or even depression.

My advice is to be yourself, but be the *best version* of yourself. You know the one I'm talking about. The you that bears the fruit of the Holy Spirit. The you that allows you to say to others, "Follow me as I follow Christ." Don't try to be something you're not.

My theology and my emotional health demand my authenticity, but so does my effectiveness. People can detect when I am not comfortable in my own skin, and that makes people nervous. If I'm trying too hard to fit, it raises questions in people's minds about my motives. Why is he trying to get me to like her? What does he *really* want? I have found that when I live out my unique God-designed version of myself, it gives others permission to do the same. When I demonstrate authentic acceptance of others, it becomes contagious. A pastor, or any other leader, can never control what people do, think or feel. Why would a good leader want to do so anyway?

But a good leader cultivates an environment where people can be themselves, bring their "stuff" to the table and be encouraged and influenced to run hard after God without being judged, dismissed, disrespected or rejected. Trust of the leader is developed in the midst of that environment of grace and freedom. When people know that their leader genuinely loves God, sincerely loves them and is ready to walk through life with them regardless of where it takes them or what they may step in along the way, they willingly allow themselves to be influenced by that leader, regardless of that leader's color, class or culture. Poser pastors are a dime a dozen and come in all shapes, sizes and *colors*. Followers can spot a phony leader a mile away, but authentic leaders will always gain an audience.

Before joining the staff of Bridgeway, I had not only become friends with senior pastor David Anderson but also with one of the associate pastors (at that time the *only* associate pastor), Dan Taylor, who among other identifying attributes, is white. When my wife, Donna, and I came to check out what God was up to in this little church, I had a candid conversation with my friend Dan. My background, experience and passion had always been primarily for student ministry, so I asked Dan about the church's students (both of them) and probed how he felt I would fit in with them, being that I am so melanin-challenged and all.

Dan made a bold statement in response to my third-degree questioning: "Mich, I have always thought that our student ministries pastor should be black." Now what was I supposed to say to that? "Fo shizzle, my brizzle! I feel ya!" Yeah right! Here's how I responded, "DT, I can be a lot of things. But I sure can't be black! I'm so white that the Beatles almost named the *White Album*, *Dave Michener*. But I am *called*. I know beyond a shadow of a doubt that God has called me to come to Bridgeway by faith to start a multicultural youth ministry where none exists. I cannot offer something I don't have, but I can offer obedience to God, passion for multicultural life and ministry, and love for the leaders of this church and the people who follow them."

Dan replied, "I know. That's why I have been praying for years for you to come here and join us in accomplishing this mission. That's why, as white as you are, man, you need to be our youth pastor." Just yesterday DT and I were having coffee and reflecting over the years of life and ministry together, and how great it is to be able to serve in a church where grace and acceptance permeates the culture—even for its *authentic* leaders.

LESSON 3: "IT" DOESN'T JUST HAPPEN

I must lead my team with intentionality when cultivating, creating and protecting a multicultural culture. The *it* is the gracist culture necessary for multicultural ministry. Gracism is a term we use around Bridgeway that is the antithesis of racism. Gracists show grace in the practical aspects of life and ministry. Gracism is to give extra goodness to those who are typically left out, marginalized or on the fringes of the dominant culture.[1]

With that being said, you can see why a multicultural church doesn't just happen. It is the result of *intentionality* in statements, staffing and prayer. At Bridgeway we wholeheartedly believe in intentionality while at the same time being open to how God's Spirit is leading. We teach intentionality when any new ministry teams form, sharing it with new team members as they are engrafted into the Bridgeway culture. We give keynote addresses, lead workshops and write about it. In *Multicultural Ministry*, David Anderson writes in detail about the importance of intentionality. Great stuff! But just when we thought we had it down, we discovered a new nuance: Don't ever assume that *everyone* gets intentionality *all* the time,

---

[1]See David A. Anderson, *Gracism: The Art of Inclusion* (Downers Grove, Ill.: InterVarsity Press, 2007).

even if they have gotten it for a long time.

The unique culture of a multicultural team must be given *constant* attention. It can never be left on autopilot. A second-tier leader or even a key ministry volunteer with a strong personality has the potential to create a following that can create a countervision and counterculture if not carefully coached. If left untended, the results can bring disunity and division to a multicultural church.

A strong culture will always assert itself, and it may surface due to the number of *people* that embrace and appreciate it. If a congregation or group is 60 percent African, then due to sheer numbers it will strongly influence the culture. This is not a bad thing, by any means, if you are trying to create a group that reflects an African culture.

When a leader has a strong *personality*, a strong culture may also surface and exert influence. A vivacious, inspiring, visionary leader, even if she or he is a lone voice at first, can swing the cultural dynamic of a group very quickly. Once a following is created, this culture can gain momentum exponentially, whether intentionally or not. Once again, this is not a bad thing if it is the kind of culture that you, the main leader, desire. But before you blink, you will have a culture on your hands that you may not want to champion.

Cultures, like gardens, need tending. I went on vacation for a few weeks this summer, and when I returned, our little garden looked very different. Lots of things were growing in it. The tomatoes, cucumbers and squash were doing okay. But the weeds were flourishing! And some of the pepper plants were gone. Rabbits had discovered our garden and enjoyed a buffet while we were at the beach. So we had to pull some weeds and put up a chicken-wire fence. We had to take out what we didn't want and protect what we did.

The same is true of tending culture. Sometimes it's not a matter of right or wrong. It's just a matter of what kind of culture you believe God wants your church to have. Another church may want the very culture you do not want, and that's okay! God uses all kinds of churches. But you are not responsible for *other* churches. You're responsible for the church *you* lead. And you must be intentional about defining the culture you want, creating a climate where that culture can flourish, and then diligently tend this culture, which will at times call for you to protect it.

Some questions. *What do you want the culture of your church to look and feel like?* Use some one-word descriptions to get started. Then let those morph into a visionary paragraph of your desired culture. (You may also want to make a similar list of what you do not want your culture to be.) Then, think of some ways you can safeguard against that in the spirit of protecting your culture.

I've learned this lesson through great successes and great failures. I was profoundly reminded that *it* does not just happen. There have been times when, due to busyness or burnout, I have allowed the cultures of different ministries to grow as they wished. They were led by good people who loved God and had great intentions. But my lack of intentional and constant gardening led to confusion and frustration. If I would have peeked at these ministries a little more often, I would have noticed their developing cultures early on and would have been able to give a more subtle and gentle redirection. Lazy leadership on my part got me an "A" in the school of hard knocks.

I have a stockpile of lessons learned. At times I permitted

frustration when it could have been prevented. I wish I could hit the rewind button and tend some ministries' cultures more intentionally.

Which ministries or leaders are influencing the culture of your church in a direction you don't want to go? What are some ways you can tend to this? A few years ago we pulled the staff together for a retreat in which we devoted a majority of the time to discussing the culture of our *church*. Using the garden analogy, we agreed that once we redefined our church's culture, we would all need to tend it in order to preserve it and allow it to flourish. So for the next year we kept coming back to what our church's culture needed to be and what weeds needed to be pulled, what ministries needed to be fertilized or pruned, and what needed to be done to allow the proper amount of sunlight and irrigation.

During that same year we began a second track of discussing the culture of our *staff*. While our church's culture had been redefined and reestablished (with hard work, prayers and tough decisions), our staff culture also needed to be tended. A leader that wants a healthy staff culture, regardless of what it looks, feels, tastes and smells like, cannot be afraid of open and honest communication. And that is what we encouraged and applauded.

Over time, with intentionality and a commitment to our mission, vision, values and *each other*, God helped us create our new *staff* culture—one that defined success as *serving* others. (I originally wrote, "we established our staff culture" but that is not accurate, and it repeats a potentially fatal error. We can't establish a garden. We plant it, tend it and watch it grow!) And God has blessed our church and staff culture in so many ways. Those stories would fill another book.

Here's a practical application: *Schedule a leadership or staff retreat*

*to discuss the topic of culture. Then come back and discuss the subject
throughout the year.*

CONCLUSION

There you have it—three simple lessons that will prepare you for
leading as a minority in a multicultural ministry. God prepared
me when there were no books to turn to such as this one. And
with Bridgeway being a place of grace for all people, including its
leaders, I have been able to practice what I preach. While God
prepared me for a ministry that most people only dream about,
there were a couple of things he did *not* prepare me for.

I was not prepared for the expression of love, acceptance and
appreciation I experience from the nonwhite people of my church.
I am affirmed more in one week of ministry at Bridgeway than I
was in a year in my unicultural (all white) church. At Bridgeway
hugs abound. Visit us sometime to see if what I'm saying isn't
true. Warning: Kisses on the cheek won't harm your skin, but
they might increase your dry-cleaning bills if you get lipstick on
your clothes.

I was not prepared for the fact that often my greatest present to
others is simply my presence. At Bridgeway our people love it
when their leaders show up at their events, whether ministry-
related or personal. At some of my other churches, when I showed
up at an event, I got the impression that they thought I was trying
to get out of work or was scoping out free food. It took me a long
time to accept the fact that people in my church (1) wanted me at
their events and (2) were actually blessed by my being there. But
it's true. Mainstream American culture values what we *do* for
people. Other cultures often value *being with* people much more
than *doing for* people.

At Bridgeway there is an incredible respect for the person leading, not simply the position itself. High value is placed on the person, and not simply because of what he or she brings to the table. People not only respect me but also heed my direction and counsel. They actually listen to me. Imagine that! I am not only permitted to lead; I'm *expected* to lead. This was a paradigm shift. My past experiences taught me that I would have to fight for every inch of leadership influence.

Please don't misunderstand what I am saying about our members. They are, as a corporate body, hands down the most gifted, skilled, intelligent, creative, successful and spirited church folks I've been around. But their respect for me as a person and my position, their expectation that I will lead, and their willingness to follow makes me want to be the best leader I can be. They deserve my best leadership efforts, and God demands my best effort.

I was not prepared for the adventure and joy that comes from living and leading in this dynamic and diverse culture. Because of Bridgeway, I will never look at life, love and leading the same way. Nor do I want to. Once you go multicultural, you'll never go back! Not this white dude, anyway.

4 PASTORAL CARE AND EDUCATION

Dan Taylor

AT THE AGE OF FOURTEEN, AT A SUMMER camp, I heard the call of God to ministry. I can still feel the cool summer night, see the stars in the sky and feel the rush of destiny I felt as I stood during the invitation to obey God. My heart and mind were never the same after that. I had gone to camp with a rebellious heart. When I arrived I remember saying to myself, *These people are* not *going to change me; they are* not *going to get to me.* I knew my parents had sent me there with hope and prayers that something would happen. Well, those *people* did not change me or get to me, but God did.

From that moment on, I focused on preparing myself with the knowledge and skills I would need to be effective in ministry. My father was a pastor of a fairly large church in upstate New York, so I became his shadow. I followed him to prisons, hospitals, psych wards, weddings, funerals and home visitation. I saw him share the gospel and lead people to Christ. We spent hours in the car, and I asked him tons of questions about theology and ministry practice. He showed me how to prepare messages. He would discuss the pastoral counseling he was doing. I attended training sessions for pastors-in-counseling. I even attended summer school at a Bible college after my junior year in high school.

Yet the idea of multicultural ministry was not on my radar. The church I grew up in was a white church. There was only one black family, and they were always in financial need. In my high school of several hundred kids, there was one African American student, and she had been adopted by a white family. In the city where our church was, the small population of African Americans all lived in the same area, which I never visited. We were cautioned that it was not safe.

Yet God was preparing me. My dad loved Jesus, yet when we would watch sporting events or news stories that had black or foreign people involved, he would make comments that made me cringe. I can't remember any of them specifically, but I do remember the heart pain I would feel when he would say them. I remember a troubled African American student who came to our youth ministry. Our youth leader and I worked hard to help him, and we tried to make him feel at home in our church community, but he never did. After several months, he left.

After graduating high school, I attended Moody Bible Institute, where my exposure to the multicultural planet we live on exploded. Moody intentionally has stayed in the middle of downtown Chicago, even though they have been offered huge tracts of rolling hills outside of the city. Moody has seized on the opportunities to train its students in the raw and real reality of city life. I remember the weird sensation the first time I found a black woman attractive! It was a reality I had never considered before. Then there was my ministry assignment was with Child Evangelism Fellowship (CEF) in inner city Chicago. This CEF experience changed me forever. I spent a year and a half ministering to over one hundred African American children, ages six to eighteen, every single week. Some of them spent a weekend on campus with me. I heard their fears, dreams, ideas of God and family, and the pain that they endured.

One of the things God taught me through those encounters and many others since then is this: "If each man or woman could understand that every other human life is as full of sorrows, or joys, or base temptations, of heartaches and of remorse as his own, . . . how much kinder, how much gentler he would be."[1]

People that are not like me have significant differences that affect how they see and interact with the world. Yet they are not weird, bizarre or wrong. They are human beings that share the same desires I do. They want to be loved; they want their families and children to be safe and to succeed in life. They want to work for a fair wage, they want to invest their lives in something bigger than themselves, and they want to be intellectually challenged and to grow. When someone they love dies, they experience the same grief I do; they celebrate when they get married and when God blesses them with children.

As different as people are, we are just as much alike as we are different. There is a common humanity that we share, regardless of culture. Yet the differences must not be ignored either. Both our common humanity and cultural diversity must be the lenses we use when providing pastoral care and adult education in a multicultural setting.

THE LANGUAGE OF PASTORAL CARE

Gary Chapman's bestselling book *The Five Love Languages* de-

---

[1]William Allen White, American newspaper editor, politician and author. *In Our Town* (New York: Macmillan, 1919), p. 363.

scribes how each person receives the message "I love you" differently. When one person has the "words of affirmation" love language and is married to someone whose love language is "acts of service," though both could be trying to communicate how much they love the other, their spouse can miss the message and actually feel unloved. Until they learn their spouse's love language and start speaking it, the message of love, no matter how sincere and well meaning, can be missed.

There is a parallel between love languages and providing both pastoral care and adult education in a multicultural congregation. We might be doing what we think is a fine job of providing care, yet we could be totally missing the mark with some of the people in our church if we don't know what their pastoral-care or education "language" is. We could be saying "I love you," but they aren't hearing anything or might conclude that we don't care about them at all. This is not just a challenge in multicultural churches. Many pastors in unicultural churches can fail as well in the eyes of their church, but the probability of this error happening in a multicultural church is multiplied by each culture represented in the congregation.

To complicate this even further, when a culture has first generation and the next generation people (referred to as "third culture kids"), each possibly having different sets of expectations, providing pastoral care for them can be very interesting![2] For example, I did a funeral of a mother from Nigeria. Some of her children still living in Nigeria flew here for the funeral. The expectations of the Nigerian children contrasted with those who had lived most of their lives in the United States. I had to learn how Nigerians think about

---

[2]First generation refers to the first generation of a family that has moved to the United States from their country of origin. Regarding "third culture kids" see David C. Pollock and Ruth E. Van Reken, *Third Culture Kids* (Boston: Nicholas Brealey, 2001).

death and what a traditional funeral is supposed to be like. Then I had to negotiate between the different desires of the two sets of children. As a pastor I hope that the death of a loved one brings about reconciliation and connection within a family, but sometimes it does not! In this instance, each group learned to honor what the other needed to make the funeral meaningful for all.

The key that helps eliminate misunderstanding, not only when an individual or family is in crisis but whenever pastoral care is appropriate, is being a learner and asking those served the best way to meet their needs. In a multicultural ministry, diverse expectations as well as theological and spiritual traditions should be *expected* and *assumed*. Expecting uniformity "because we are all Christians" is immature and shortsighted. God does not fit into the boxes we have created for him, and his people are no different!

I'm not saying we have to meet all expectations. While some can be met, others cannot. Sometimes accommodations can be made by referring to others who might be able to meet a member's needs when our church is not able or equipped to do so. There are times when it is appropriate to educate church members about biblical principles that might guide them in the actions they should take; this might challenge their expectations and cultural norms. Yet the key is communicating, sometimes overcommunicating, to make sure both sides understand each other. This is more difficult with cultures who have difficulty asking for help or are resistant even after we have asked. I find this especially true with some of the Asian cultures. If I suspect this is happening, I phone a pastor or another member of our church from that culture and ask what is the normal cultural expectation. I then approach the family to see if what was suggested is something they would like the church to do for them.

THE BIBLICAL FOUNDATION OF MINISTERING TO THE BODY

Before we get into specifics of pastoral care and education, I believe that it is important to look at some of the biblical foundations for them.

The dominant Greek word we translate as "to minister" is *diakoneō* (noun form is *diakonos*). The etymology of this word literally means "to wait on tables." The English word *deacon* comes from the Latin translation of the word. In its various forms this root word results in many different English words. Some of them in the NIV are *service, mission, wait on tables, to help, servant* (Mark 9:35), *minister, ministry* (2 Timothy 4:5), *promotes* (Galatians 2:17), *helpful* (2 Timothy 4:11), *ministering, serving* (1 Peter 1:12).

Though the word *deacon* can have a very specific meaning in certain Christian traditions—in my history, it was the guys in charge of the church leadership (see 1 Timothy 3:8-12)—in the biblical text it is a generic word meaning to serve an individual or group, meeting their physical or spiritual needs. It is not predominately about a position but an activity. A person doesn't have to be a paid staff member or even have the title "minister" to do the work of a minister. I wonder whether we should use the term "pastoral care" since it implies care that only a pastor can give. Maybe "ministry care," "body care," "church care" or "serving care" would be better. When we serve the body of Christ and the broken world around us, especially in the way God has shaped us,[3] we *are* ministers.

When ministering to someone, we cannot have the "this is the way I was trained to do this" mentality. *We need humility and the heart of a student to truly be effective ministers, regardless of our de-*

---

[3]See Erik Rees, *S.H.A.P.E.: Finding and Fulfilling Your Unique Purpose for Life* (Grand Rapids: Zondervan, 2006).

grees and training. If we approach a multicultural congregation with the attitude of "I know how to do this," we severely cut our ability to touch and reach them.

To minister biblically we must invest our time learning from others, reading and listening—truly listening—to the hearts and the words of those we serve. We will ask basic questions and be careful not to make assumptions.[4] In many ways we do the work and learning of a missionary, not for the purpose of evangelism (non-Christians) but to serve the body (Christians). Only God can meet certain needs, but as we minister to others, we still are responsible to petition God on their behalf to meet their need.

But how do we know we have truly ministered to others? When they feel better? The funeral or wedding or house blessing went well? They say we did? Those might be helpful, but I believe we have truly ministered when people are connected to Christ as the one who will meet their needs and is the source of their strength and perseverance (2 Corinthians 9:8; Philippians 4:10-13; 1 Timothy 5:5; Hebrews 4:14-16; 7:22-26, 2 Peter 1:3). This doesn't mean that the body of Christ isn't a part of the process. It can and often should be (Acts 2:44-45; Romans 12:13; 2 Corinthians 8:10-14; Ephesians 4:28; Philippians 4:16; 1 Timothy 5:16; Titus 3:13). But we often look to people as the *ultimate* source of meeting our needs, and use God as a backup 911 call. Our culture has abandoned God as its "need meeter," so we look to others—government, charities, churches or communities—for help. Often, without thinking, Christians fall into this pattern, often placing all their hopes on the pastor showing up or the church giving them a loan. Again, the church should reach out and help

---

[4]In cognitive-based therapy making assumptions is called "mind reading." See David C. Burns, *The Feeling Good Handbook* (New York: Penguin Putnam, 1999), p. 9.

where and when it can, but it must not take the place of God as the source of all good things. The church only reflects the goodness of God as it helps others.

A final word to ministers, whether staff or volunteers. Meeting people's needs feels good. It makes us feel worthwhile, significant. The problem comes when we become addicted to that feeling.[5] There is a way of serving that is totally selfish. We can't *use* people, especially people in need, to make *us* feel better. Fulfillment is there, but it is not our motivation for reaching out to people and helping them in times of need or crisis.

Personal motives can become toxic when ministering. We may *want* others to be dependent on us, to see *us* as meeting all their needs. When we succumb to this temptation, we turn others into idolaters—we become their "graven image." As a pastor I have to fight this battle everyday. People *have* to talk to me; someone *has* to see me. No, they don't. If I can see them, I most certainly will; but when I am constantly running to meet needs and take every phone call and make all the hospital visits, I am in enemy territory. When I *need* to do all that, I have to question my own ministry motives. I might not be ministering to them, I might be trying to lure them into depending on me. That is a fearful way to treat God's people, because he is watching. (Read Ezekiel 34 for a sobering message.)

ADULT EDUCATION

I love to teach. I could do it every day and never get tired of it. When I was in sixth or seventh grade, I remember teaching my peers on the book of Revelation! I was totally juiced by the experi-

---

[5]Anne Jackson, *Mad Church Disease* (Grand Rapids: Zondervan, 2009); Kent and Barbara Hughes, *Liberating Ministry from the Success Syndrome* (Wheaton, Ill.: Tyndale House, 1987); and Charles Swindoll, *Improving Your Serve* (Waco, Tex.: Word, 1981).

ence and I was good at it. My father was a great model of passionate teaching. Yet teaching is not *about* or *for* the teacher, but the learners.

Confusing knowledge with maturity. In segments of American church culture, some have replaced spiritual maturity with biblical knowledge and the elevation of teachers. The assumption is that those with more biblical and theological knowledge are spiritually mature. I fear that many have their faith in knowledge of the Bible, but not in God. They worship knowledge or the Bible, not God. Please don't misunderstand: biblical knowledge is critical for spiritual growth, but it is not the measure of spiritual maturity. As one of my Bible college professors said, "Truth that has not been lived has not been learned." Many American Christians are long on knowledge and short on application.

Biblically relevant teaching. One of the joys of teaching in a multicultural setting is that most other cultures are primarily interested in application. They might find the current archaeology of the city of Jericho interesting for about fifty seconds, but then they want to know how to apply the Joshua story. Being a teacher in a multicultural congregation has pushed me to a more balanced approach to teaching.

In one of my early teaching opportunities at Bridgeway I used the word *Pentateuch* and hands immediately shot up in the air. "What does the word *Pentateuch* mean?" Wow, for a white kid raised in a Baptist church, I cut my theological teeth on Christian vocabulary. At Bridgeway I don't "dumb down" my instruction, but just as in a children's ministry we must have "age-appropriate" education, with adults we need to have "biblically relevant" teaching.

Knowing the word *Pentateuch* is not going to change people's lives, yet teaching them how to read the Old Testament as a life-long skill will. As teachers we must lay aside our desire to regurgitate all we know, and only teach stuff that will enlighten others' spiritual journeys. This takes as much listening as speaking. (For the more knowledge-driven in class, I always provide footnotes or a booklist for further study.)

The main focus of my teaching is on new actions, perspectives, skills and habits that will move people toward Christ. For example, I once taught on the phrase "pray without ceasing." I began by focusing on the omnipresence of God, spending most of the time helping the class think through how God's omnipresence connects to prayer as spiritual breathing. (I was prepared to teach more on the omnipresence of God if the group wasn't sure they believed it or never had heard of it. This puts more pressure on me to prepare, but that is my job.)

I subscribe to this principle: *The teacher has not taught or is not finished teaching if the students have not learned.*[6] The main way to know whether students have learned is if they make life and perspective changes based on your instruction, *not* if they have filled in all the blanks in their notes.

Interactive learning. Adult education needs to be interactive. We must get the students talking to us and to one another. Many times, instead of looking up all the passages about a subject myself, I divide the students into small groups and assign passages for them to investigate. Yes, sometimes it is a pooling of biblical ignorance, but those are teaching moments we can seize upon. And the students will remember not just the content of the lesson, but they will also develop Bible-reading and study skills. Design lessons with less verbal time for you and more exploration and interaction for them. I call this "cross discipleship": they are not

---

[6]See Josh Hunt and Dr. Larry Mays, *Disciple-Making Teachers* (Loveland, Colo.: Group, 1998).

dependent totally on me but learn from one another. I serve more as a guide than a teacher. It does at times feel like herding cats, but the energy that comes out of these interactive sessions stay with them longer than a notebook full of filled-in blanks.

For example, I was teaching a group of potential small group leaders. Instead of the traditional way of teaching—"This is how you lead a small group"—I treated them as a small group for several sessions so they experienced the kind of small group I wanted them to reproduce. Then after three weeks of experience, I used those weeks as an illustration of how I wanted them to lead small groups. Since they experienced it themselves, it was no longer mere ideas and theories. They had a feel for what a good small group experience is supposed to be. Finally, before the training was finished, each of them led the rest of us through a small group session. I then coached them with feedback after it was over.[7]

Intrinsic motivation. The individual in an adult education setting has to be intrinsically motivated or the personal investment is not there. I'm sure I'm not the only pastor who has someone bring up an issue they are struggling with or wish they knew more about, and thought to myself, *We just spent the last three months covering that, and you were there!* Before, it was just information, but now—when they are internally motivated—they seek life change.

I recently met with a guy at Starbucks who spent most of his life as an atheist, but through the testimony of his wife and a men's small group he has moved from atheism to a combination of theism and deism. Sending him to the traditional learning venues of our church is not going to help him. I sent him ten book titles,

---

[7]I appreciate the situational leadership model, which woke me up to this approach. See Ken Blanchard, *Self-Leadership and the One-Minute Manager* (New York: HarperCollins, 2005), and Thom and Joani Schultz, *Why Nobody Learns Much of Anything at Church: And How to Fix It* (Loveland, Colo.: Group, 1996).

asking him to pick the one he found most interesting. We will read and talk about the book he chose. He is internally motivated to learn, to begin a "spiritual education." So I tapped into what he was interested in. Sometimes this kind of exercise leads to an area that I haven't had a lot of exposure to! It forces me as the teacher/instructor to stretch myself. I know without a doubt that the next three months we spend reading and talking—and I will be fervently praying, depending on God to work with us—will do more for his spiritual knowledge and progress than a whole year of the normal kind of instruction that most churches offer.

I realize we cannot teach every person one-on-one. Yet instead of being locked into a teaching regimen that you "have to do" because "we have always done this," how about sensing what God is doing in your congregation week by week, creating teaching venues and events that strike at what is currently taking place? This will free you up to do more informal teaching as well.

CONCLUSION

In the movie *Love Actually* two characters meet in a country home in France. Jamie is British writer. Aurelia is the Portuguese housekeeper. A romance blooms though neither speaks the other's language, they have no way to share how they feel. When Jamie returns to London, unknown to Aurelia, he starts to learn Portuguese, and unknown to him, she learns English. On Christmas Eve he flies back to France, hunts her down at a restaurant and in his newly learned Portuguese expresses his emotions to her and asks her to marry him. In her faltering English she answers yes.

What I love about the story is that the motivation to communicate with the other was so powerful they were willing to submit to a learning process. American spiritual leaders can learn from

Jamie and Aurelia. Investing the time to learn about other cultures and how to care for and educate people from these cultures is what loving Christ is about. Jamie and Aurelia were motivated by love, and many times I have to look in the mirror and ask, *Do I love the church of Christ, more than myself?* If the answer is yes, then what cost am I willing to pay, what effort am I willing to extend to express the love of Christ to his church?

I have learned from traveling to other parts of the world and experiencing the universal body of Christ. It has broadened my narrow American perspective of the church. The church is a dynamic, swirling, impossible-to-box, beautiful expression of God. We leaders are asked to care for, teach, lead and love Christ's bride. May that love form the church into the image of Christ, instead of trying to form it into *our* image.

CREATIVE ARTS AND MULTICULTURAL MINISTRY

Rich Becker

I REMEMBER THE MOMENT ALMOST TWO decades ago that the young David Anderson put his arm around me, after we had finished a church event, and said, "Rich, couldn't you do this your whole life?" Laughing, I looked at him and walked away, but then I realized he was serious. In the weeks and months that followed, David continued to inquire, following the Spirit, and officially invited me to join him in his church planting adventure in the suburbs of Washington, D.C.

I resisted following because I had CMD. I admit it, growing up I developed "Church Ministry Dysfunction." Perhaps you have experienced this as well. I based my earliest beliefs about ministry on local churches across the country led by preachers that were unskilled in teaching or plain burned out. Most of these churches had music programs of poor quality, outdated or poorly operated sound equipment, and uncomfortable pews or folding chairs. And they were unicultural. The church experience was uneventful, boring and irrelevant.

Thus, I didn't even want to invite my friends to my own church, because frankly I was embarrassed by it. I didn't want to be associated with "church," but God had other plans. My first insights into creativity and the church being compatible occurred when attending Willow Creek Community Church, and this went far toward healing my CMD. I had always been driven to incorporate emerging media in the arts, but it was not until David asked me to join him that I began to see the work God had already begun in my heart. That invitation put a spotlight on a growing desire to do church in a different way, a way that would not be embarrassing and utilized my own passion for cutting-edge technology. After much prayer and soul searching, I felt called to move from Chicago, where I grew up and planned to live the rest of my life, to the Washington, D.C., area, where Bridgeway Community Church would soon be.

> What was your church experience? What beliefs did you form about church growing up?
>
> Are you aware of how your beliefs about church affect your participation in ministry today?
>
> Are you willing to have your beliefs challenged, possibly even letting them go?

IT'S NOT JUST CHURCH—IT'S *BRIDGEWAY!*

My personal call from God was not to just start a church, but one that would embrace the arts, pay attention to quality and be a place people could comfortably invite others. I was no longer able to deny my passion to do church creatively. However, I learned rather quickly that my call and David's call were not the same.

My desire was to start a church that focused on creative arts, but David's call was to plant a church that would truly be multicultural. While this could have been devastating to us (and the revelation did not come quickly), we eventually learned through the growth and development of the church that our calls could coexist. With obedience came the realization that God had truly called us to the same thing. The key to embracing many cultures in one church is to be creative and dynamic!

Is your whole team committed to the same vision?

Is your vision broad enough to encompass all that God intends for the ministry he is calling your church to?

In our case, God placed a seemingly full vision in each of our hearts, bringing us together to fully form his vision. Is there a specific God-given vision on your heart that may require obedient representation in spite of strong voices having seemingly different calls?

BUILDING A MULTICULTURAL CREATIVE-ARTS MINISTRY

Prioritize values. God First! Before Bridgeway came to be, it was a hope and a promise. The first step in realizing the ministry was to figure out what our priorities were. This was especially important since each team member represented a part of the vision. We established together that above all else, we wanted to honor God

What are the top priorities of your ministry?

Have you communicated this to your staff or leadership team? How?

and be biblical. Second, our platform, our stage and our services had to be multicultural. The values of excellence and quality naturally came successively.

Create a safe environment. Setting a multicultural stage by utilizing diverse servants and leaders is obviously critical, but to have diverse services your planning team must be diverse also. Putting a multicultural face on something monolithic will not necessarily produce culturally diverse services. The best way to ensure you are incorporating diverse and relevant elements is to begin at the planning stage. Maintaining a safe environment when building a creative arts planning team is essential. Your team must feel safe and comfortable enough to voice their opinions, speak up without fear of retaliation or damaged relationships, and each feel their contribution is valid and valuable to the group—no matter how creatively outrageous it may sound. We have learned that this requires a willingness to freely give grace to one another, even with racial issues. Make sure you have "safe people" who will be honest with you and tell you the truth, who have the freedom to share without fear of offending or being offended.

Is your team filled with "safe people" who feel safe and who others feel safe around?

Do you have safe people you can go to when you are trying something out before it hits the stage?

Are you asking questions of others like, "I have this idea I am thinking about doing, what do you think?" Are you asking the people who are different than you?

What have you done or can you do to maintain a safe environment for your team?

Form your team. The more diverse the contributions of the planning team are, the better! Without compromising safety in the team, intentionally have people on the team who have different views, are of a different race and have different styles than you. One person on my team for many years always wanted to include video and drama elements that pushed the envelope beyond what is traditionally acceptable in church. We had to use him sparingly as a service producer because his style was so identifiable. But his contribution to the planning team as a whole was always very helpful. He contributed a perspective we would not have understood or represented otherwise. However, it was vital to have other perspectives equally represented to balance the team.

When someone on your team is edgy and out of the box, it is helpful to also have someone more conservative who is able to ground certain elements. Having these conversations with people different than you opens the door for constructive criticism; when allowed, this fleshing out of ideas can balance what you offer to your congregation.

Lead your team. Having diverse viewpoints from your team members enhances the creative process. However, with diverse viewpoints comes the potential for divergent or competing ideas and values. It is the role of the leader to balance the cultures and styles within the team, and to make sure this does not become contentious. When conflict does arise, we have discovered that relationships are the key to diffusing tension and refocusing our eyes on the ministry. Personal and trusting relationships must exist between team members and also between the leader and each member. This requires strong leadership.

If there is conflict between two of our team members and the relationship and respect for one another is not enough to overcome the offense, it is often my personal relationship with the team members that alleviates the conflict and prevents the problems from escalating further. Good relationships build creativity and security within the team, which allows you to plan effective services that are relevant to each culture you are trying to reach with the Word. It is important that each member feels the leader understands his or her view, style and culture. Members must be able to trust that their interest is protected, especially when it is not chosen for a particular service or element of the service.

When these relationships are established, potential disaster can be averted. In one of the scenes of a show we did, I addressed a male African American actor as "boy." At the time, I did not know this word could be interpreted as racially motivated. I was pulled aside after the rehearsal by the senior pastor, who, knowing me, knew I had not intended to highlight or address this particular racial slur nor to offend, but had spoken out of ignorance. If we had gone ahead into live production without having been made aware of the potential hurtfulness, the use of this seemingly innocuous word would have distracted from the message we intended. For anyone in our congregation who has been or is still affected by this issue, this word likely would have taken them "out" for several minutes. For this reason it is very important to know what you are saying and be cautious not to draw attention to controversial racial issues if you are not prepared to flesh it out or intend to address it.

This scenario could have gone very differently had our relationship and understanding not been fully established beforehand. Grace was imparted at every step. Because of our relationship, the senior pastor was able to overcome any offense he may have felt in the moment, know my intent and communicate what he suspected to be the case; he knows and trusts me as a leader. He encouraged me and educated me without admonishing or judging me, and in return grace was administered again in the receiving of the message. Because I know he has my best interest at heart, I did not take offense at his correction.

Some things will get by your planning team. It is impossible to know all possible racially contentious words and phrases, and to only be purposeful in usage. This is why it is important to have safe people around you. They will cover you because they know you are committed to racial reconciliation. Abound with grace. Take heed of advice and cautions as they come, and be thankful for the people who are brave enough to speak out. Having checkpoints with safe relationships is necessary throughout the creative planning process and even into production.

THE CREATIVE PROCESS

Boundless creativity. Having created a safe environment for your diverse team, you can then fully jump unhindered into the creative process. We have found that embracing all ideas and not dismissing any is a helpful foundation to creative planning. Creativity builds on itself. Even the farthest stretching ideas can inspire a new direction as long as it is valued and not judged. Encourage your team to identify what works in every idea offered; don't shut down the creativity just because the whole concept cannot work. Good leadership in creative planning lifts the limits. The team must be able to be in the moment and unhindered in the creative process. The creative arts leader must be responsible to keep sight of the big picture, bringing it back into focus as an idea is developed and an element is produced.

Don't play it too safe! The creative arts director must take some calculated risks. The growth of the congregation comes from educating and bringing exposure to cultural issues. If the team is not riding the edge or pushing the envelope, there is a risk of stagnating. These risks must sometimes be taken even in the face of some advisers being unsure. Keep in mind that changing a few words or fleshing out an idea until the intent is clearly recognized as nonprovocative can sometimes avoid the sting of an issue. It is not necessary to always discard an element because it might possibly hurt somebody's feelings.

Grow and adapt. When Bridgeway began, there were four of us before we were thousands. I played the piano for our worship time, and I was hands down the best! Or rather, the best we had. As our ministry grew, better alternatives developed. Creative arts ministry is an art form, but it may not be possible to foster excellence and diversity prior to growth occurring. In early stages everyone's stage presence may not be on par. Some people may believe I never was, but we had to allow the bar of excellence to rise as the Lord brought more talent to the church. When we grew, my level of talent was no longer appropriate. This continues to happen as we balance quality and intentionality.

When we began, we offered everyone the opportunity to serve in creative arts. For example, the choir was open to all. As we grew, however, this had to be adjusted. We are unable to accommodate the sheer numbers of people desiring to serve on stage. We want each person to utilize their unique gifts and have created opportunities for this. Yet we have not discovered how to allow everyone who wants to participate in stage ministry to do so as consistently as we would like. This phase of growth has come with growing pains. We must continually adjust not only to greater talent but also to greater racial diversity. When a servant no longer fits either the race component needed or the quality desired, rebalancing is rarely easy. It is important to communicate clearly and in love the reasons why rebalancing is necessary. Once again, the relationship between the leader and the team member plays a vital role in maintaining the unity of the ministry while growing in excellence.

KEY COMPONENTS FOR A DYNAMIC MULTICULTURAL PRODUCTION

Intentionality on stage. I will let you in on an important little secret: Intentionality really starts with Sunday morning services. I am not sure who said it first, but I've heard Bill Hybels say, "As goes Sunday, so goes the church." The Sunday morning service is our front door, it is the first point of entry with few exceptions, and what we look like is the first and most formative impression of who we are. What happens on Sunday drives what happens in the rest of the church. Sunday services, including ministry announcements, are the church's primary communication tool, so all ministries build from this foundation. Without a multicultural congregation, it would be difficult, if not impossible, to build a racially diverse men's ministry, community outreach ministry or any other ministry.

Fortunately for us, we were multicultural from day one: David is black, his wife Asian, and my wife and I are white. We were the church and were determined to grow, but grow with diversity. We recognized early in the process that racial diversity would not happen without intentionally fostering it. It will not happen by accident . . . ever!

One of the great byproducts of being a multicultural church is that interracial couples feel comfortable. Often they cannot go to a black church or a white church because one of them feels alienated at either. At Bridgeway we have seen a huge influx of interracial couples, so we have embraced this on our stage too. If a drama sketch includes a married or dating couple, we often use actors from different races to play the couple. We don't do this to have race as a discussion topic but simply to reflect our congregation. Sometimes we run into casting issues when these couples are scripted to have children; we use kids of one race or the other rather than trying to find "believable" biracial kids. The audience has been trained to "suspend disbelief."

> Does your stage reflect the diversity you currently have in your congregation or the diversity you want to have in your congregation?

Know your audience. Knowing who is in your audience is as important as knowing who you put on stage. This is critical. Race has been such a divisive issue for such a long time that people are still sensitive to it. While we believe racial diversity leads to a beautiful combination of people, we understand there may be people in our congregation who are not racially reconciled because of their own experiences of racism or the way they were raised to view people of other races. We do not want to produce something that will throw people off track with what we present on stage. Ultimately, our desire is for people to come into a relationship with Christ.

Bridgeway is extremely diverse and our mission has been clearly communicated from the pastors, on our website and in all our publications. We have worked hard to demonstrate honor for all peoples. Because of this, we have the privilege of making light of cultures and races in a way that is not offensive. Our audience does not call our intentions into question, because they understand our heart for bringing people of all backgrounds together through the gospel message of Jesus Christ. One year our Christmas production was a sitcom about an interracial couple, a black female and a white male, coming together for Christmas for the first time with their families. The set up allowed us to include racial humor, but poking fun at the stereotypes was only acceptable because of where we were as a church. Had we been a white church with a few black people or a black church with a few white people, this humor would not have gone over well. You must be careful to know your audience while taking creative risks with racial comments, humor and statements. There is a great place for this in appreciating and enjoying each other's cultures, but you must be mindful to not cause offense.

In your desire to be multicultural and to recognize racial stereotypes, find ways to move your congregation to this change. Calculated risks are worth taking and can be effective and non-overt teaching tools in cultural education.

In addition to racial differences, it is also important to recognize people's church history. In our nondenominational setting, attendees come from a wide variety of church backgrounds and may be used to hymns, a certain style of dress, a certain way of coming to the altar or how the offering is taken. It is really important that we pay attention to all the different backgrounds. We want to give honor and credence to people's church history while still being multicultural and contemporary, so we make sure we have variety within the main service: contemporary music and old hymns, different styles of teachers, different forms of dance—all inclusive of the cultures our congregation represents. Dividing these elements into separate themed services (i.e., traditional, contemporary, etc.) may appear to suit the needs of the congregation, particularly in a unicultural setting, but in a multicultural setting we fear it would create a hindrance to true diversity and our core value of reconciliation. We continue to hold racial diversity as a high value, and this necessitates an obvious balancing act. While it has gotten easier with time, intentionally creating a colorful stage requires continual effort.

Set the stage (staging). Because we first want to honor God and be true to what the Bible says, we decided that honoring diversity is more important than performance excellence. You can imagine the struggles that this sometimes creates, even jealousy, among servants. For example, one person might know that he or she is the better choice (based on skill) for a specific song, drama part or dance, and yet someone of a different race, age or gender got the part because of our desire for diversity on the stage. Our distribution of stage time can feel unfair and even exploitive to some, but being multicultural does not happen by accident.

Conversations about staging and intentionality are not few and far between. We have had to learn to communicate and support our vision to those who do not understand. Accusations of affirmative action, not honoring the call of God on a servant's life and just plain racial insensitivity all necessitate difficult conversations, which do not always end with hugs. Some people never see the value of our vision. When someone continually questions the mission, vision and values of our church, we encourage him or her to consider looking for a place that fits their unique composition and call. We believe in the greater body of Christ, and in no way feel that a person is ungodly if they are called to another church, even though these partings can be painful.

A leader in a multicultural church must firm up the decision to choose intentionality in staging above being popular, must trust God to bring the right people and must be certain of the calling.

Are you certain of your own call?

Are you ready to make hard choices to defend the vision in the face of accusation?

Do you have the support of your leadership in doing so?

Maintain communication and trust. One clear aspect of the success of any multicultural creative arts ministry is making sure the senior pastor and the creative arts, or worship, director are in clear communication. This will help maintain the unity of and preserve trust in the whole church's ministry. David and I had to figure out how we could trust each other and communicate well. Once we were able to align our goals to become a multicultural creative arts church, communication became much easier, but our learning to trust each other's decisions, even though he is the boss and I am his subordinate, is vital. David often told me that any good subordinate knows how to lead up, being able to respectfully lead your boss in the direction you want to go. This understanding eventually paved a path for agreement between us.

When pastors and creative arts directors are not on the same page, elements of distrust and disunity are fostered. We have learned that unity requires trust. In churches that have this kind of tension, it often seems to perpetuate a dual church experience, causing the creative arts ministry to separate from the main message if there is not a common theme. This effect is more divisive than attractive.

When the creative arts team makes decisions about casting and directing a service with excellence and quality, David must be certain that our first desire is to have a multicultural stage that honors God. This trust allows grace in times when he does not see the complete diversity he would like, and this grace protects the creative process. Our first order of excellence is racial diversity, so our pastor can know with assurance that it was simply not possible if it is not present.

A WORD TO SENIOR PASTORS

If you are a senior pastor or leader who has creative arts people or worship leaders reporting to you, keep in mind that what they do is art as well as ministry. Their pride in producing art must be honored. It is also a vulnerability that has to be nurtured. They put as much care into their art as you do in your preaching and teaching. Creative people feel the need to take risks, which needs to be honored and encouraged.

Creative arts ministry will not work without allowing someone to fail. It may be difficult as a senior leader to see something go down or go bad. The ability or freedom to take risks and succeed or fail are important if you want to cultivate a community of artists. This freedom to fail will allow your creative ministry to grow to the next level of God-glorifying excellence.

THE PRODUCT

Putting it all together—the vision, the team, the staging, "the show"—can seem like a daunting task. With so many variables and people to consider, it can be hard work making it to Sunday. The redeeming quality of it all is that once your Sunday comes (and goes) your team will have created a space where those gathered are free to worship our good Father in a new and dynamic way amidst a body of believers that reflects God's own heart to draw all people to himself. It is a blessing to serve a creative and artistic God.

Chad's Story

Picture a bright red pickup truck with a giant Nebraska Cornhuskers sticker on the back window pulling into your church parking lot. Now picture the driver. His name is Chad. He's about 5'11" tall and loves going to the theater to watch Shakespeare's plays. He attended predominantly white churches with his family growing up, spending some time in Methodist and Baptist congregations. Can you picture him?

I bet you can't. Chad is a living oxymoron. He is half Lakota Sioux Native American and half black, was raised by his white adoptive parents and culturally identifies himself more with white culture. People typically think Chad is an African American when they first see or meet him. He is quick to correct them, because he is extremely proud of what he considers his three ethnic heritages.

Chad was at a bookstore in Columbia one night when he saw Dr. David Anderson promoting the book *Letters Across the Divide*. Chad bought the book and read it when he got home. Learning that Dr. Anderson's church was in the town he lived in, Chad decided to pay a visit to Bridgeway. Immediately he noticed it was unlike any church he had ever attended. He remembers, "I liked it, but it was unusual. I was not accustomed to multicultural churches. It was unique, but I loved it from the beginning."

At that time, Chad was engaged to his now wife, Tanisha,

who grew up in a black Pentecostal church environment. What appealed to Chad about Bridgeway was that it was able to blend their two different church backgrounds. Chad says, "The intentional multicultural vision wholeheartedly influenced our decision to make Bridgeway our church home."

For a long time, Chad thought everyone's church experience was like his. When he learned this was not the case, he struggled with questions like, "Why do blacks have to be so loud or emotional in church?" After attending Bridgeway for almost seven years, Chad feels he has become much more aware and sensitive to other cultures and has a better understanding of the cultural reasons for what they do. Even though ethnically Chad is half black, his experience being part of an intentionally multicultural church has helped him improve his relationships with other black people.

Many elements of Bridgeway's multicultural approach were new to Chad when he first arrived. He was unaccustomed to the style of music that was more upbeat than the traditional style of songs he grew up singing in church. He was not used to clapping his hands during worship. But worshiping next to other people of color was the biggest change of all. This is now what Chad enjoys most about his Bridgeway experience. Whenever he is away and visits another church, he "misses seeing all the different colors and cultures" and being around different kinds of people.

"I love Bridgeway. I love what it has brought to me, to my wife and to my daughter. It has enriched our lives. It has made us more open and willing to build bridges and relationships with others. It has been great. It has been uncomfortable at times, but that's how we grow."

MULTICULTURAL WORSHIP

Nikki Lerner

ONCE MY HUSBAND AND I WERE ENGAGED, one of the biggest decisions that we had to make was where we would attend church. The church I had been attending for four years prior to our engagement was a large, predominantly white, Pentecostal church in the Baltimore suburbs. It was a wonderful place where I began maturing in my journey with Christ and becoming a fully devoted follower of Christ. The church that my then fiancé attended was a small church of about thirty people and was also predominantly white (well, they did have one black guy). While we were dating, neither one of us were very comfortable at the other's church homes. This was a problem, since we thought it important to attend the same church fellowship once we were married.

I will never forget one of the first times that we attended a service together at my home church. I remember turning to David during the worship and asking, "What do you think?" His response was, "Where are all of the black people?" I was very confused. I said, "What do you mean? I'm right here!" This would turn out to be a situation that was not easily fixed. You see, we are an interracially mixed couple. David is white, and I am black. So, you might imagine why I was confused by his earlier question. He, as a white man, felt very uncomfortable in a place that was not racially mixed. Furthermore, he shared with me that he wanted to find a church where we did not stand out. Where people would not stare at us when we walked by. A place where, if we chose to have children, they would see other children that looked like them and would not feel out of place. He asked that we find a new place to worship together. So, where would you find such a place? I had never seen a place like he had described. The search was on.

I remember, fondly, the day that we walked into a service at Bridgeway Community Church. It was the first time I had walked into a place where I saw people of different races and backgrounds worshiping together. The most amazing thing I saw that day was interracially mixed couples like us! I couldn't believe it. We walked into the service and felt right at home. No one stared at us, no one seemed surprised by the way that we looked as a couple. This was new. This was right. And this was even before the actual service began! Once the service began, the band and the singers led us in singing and praise. I was blown away. What I saw on stage was the same thing that I saw in the congregation itself. People of different races worshiping together, playing music with one another, smiling and enjoying one another. We were hooked. We had found a home at Bridgeway Community Church.

A lot has happened since that first Sunday in 1999. I have had the privilege to learn from our pastors, teachers and worship leaders about what it means to live, love and thrive in a multicultural setting.

I began singing in the worship ministry and began serving as a part of the worship leadership team in 2000. After years of serving in the worship ministry and even serving on staff at Bridge-way as a pastoral assistant, in 2007 God called me to lead the worship ministry itself. I am the worship leader/director of a won-derfully diverse ministry. I have the pleasure of serving and lead-ing a growing ministry of roughly one hundred people. We have a diverse team of musicians and vocalists that call Bridgeway home and who serve together to lead people to a deeper relation-ship with God through song. I have the responsibility of making sure that when people walk into our church, they feel welcomed and see their own race and culture lifted up.

Our worship ministry has a significant impact on our church and the community around us, not only in worship but in racial reconciliation and harmony. When was the last time you walked into a church and saw a stage full of racially diverse musicians and singers? When was the last time you went to a Christian concert and saw a team of racially diverse musicians and singers praising God? Unfortunately, this is hard to come by. When people see our ministry, they are reminded of what the kingdom of God is sup-posed to look like. People from every nation and culture and age group worshiping God *together.*

Your church can experience the joy and freedom of worshiping in a racially and culturally diverse setting. I hope you are able to take some of the things that I have learned while doing worship and music ministry at Bridgeway and apply them in your own context.

WORSHIP MINISTRY IMPACT IN A MULTICULTURAL SETTING

For your multicultural worship ministry to have an impact on your congregation as well as your community, you must be inten-tional about what you produce for people to hear and see, and be sensitive to the cultural dynamics of your congregation.

What is seen. When my husband and I walked through the doors of Bridgeway, the first experience we had was what we *saw*. Don't underestimate the power of what is seen in ministry. Let me explain.

When the worship and music began, the first thing that we saw were people of different races walking onstage. The drummer and bass player were Filipino, the guitar player and keyboardist were white. The singers were white, black and Asian. The worship leader was black. Before they even played a note or sang a lyric, I was ministered to. Why? Because someone thought enough of me, a black woman, walking through the door to know that I needed to see someone on the stage that looked like me. This is critical. Chances are that the singers and musicians are the first team that your congregation sees when the service begins. Your team sets the stage (no pun intended) for what the church is all about, and this is even before one note is played or sung.

Key 1: Build multicultural teams. Excellence is one of the values of both Bridgeway and the worship ministry. For our ministry, *diversity is equivalent to excellence*. If there is no diversity, then we have not hit the excellence mark. That is how important this first principle is to us.

One of the easiest ways to elevate the value of diversity is to build multicultural teams. When thinking through your band and singing rotations, always look through the lens of diversity. Protect it at all costs. Be creative. Think outside the box. For example, we would never put an all–African American worship team on stage. Why? Because presenting a unicultural worship team of any kind does not lift up the value of diversity.

Having an all–African American team of singers in a multicultural congregation wouldn't communicate to our congregation that all are welcome and all have a voice. Some may counter that people are people, so what is the big deal? The big deal is that if my husband and I walked into Bridgeway in 1999 and saw an all–African American worship team, we might assume that Bridgeway was an African American church. To us, as an interracial couple, we may not have felt safe or part of the church, from the standpoint of diversity. The congregation may have been mixed, but we might have assumed that the African American culture held the most influence.

When a church has a team of different races leading the congregation with one voice, the congregation gets the message that all cultures have a voice in that ministry. When you choose singers and musicians for your teams and rotations, be sure to consider the racial makeup of those teams. If your drummer and bass player are white, then the rest of your band needs to be more diverse. Find people of other races to be the keyboardist and guitar player. If necessary, find someone—maybe someone from another ministry—to play with the band to uphold the value of racial diversity. If you are the *main* worship leader and are Asian, make sure that you choose a person of another race as an associate worship leader. Building multicultural teams is a sure way to uphold the value of diversity in your worship ministry.

Key 2: Create an atmosphere of diverse worship expression. The Western church seems to have constant wars about "worship expression," that is, how we as people physically respond to God during our worship. For example, some people lift their hands during worship when they feel connected to God. Some who are a bit more reserved simply close their eyes when worshiping. Others shout and yell when responding to God. And some even dance a little.

In a multicultural church, it is critical for the worship leader to create and encourage an atmosphere of diverse worship expression. The congregation needs to know and to *see* that it is okay to respond to God in various ways. Sometimes assumptions are made about the way different races respond to God during times of musical worship and singing. There are plenty of stereotypes. White people and Asian people are more reserved and want to listen passively, don't want to move with the music, like music that is driven by acoustic guitars only, and like to clap on beats 1 and 3. Black people and Hispanic people love to scream, shout and fall on the floor during worship services; their music is more lively and keyboard driven, and they like to sing things over and over again in their worship.

While there may be elements of truth to these stereotypes, it is critical to be aware that all of these worship expressions may occur in a multicultural setting. And that's okay. It's okay to create an atmosphere for people to be free to respond as God has wired them and to be comfortable with how their own culture has influenced their response to God in worship. It's not the worship leader's job to manipulate or tell people how to respond to God; we want the Holy Spirit to move the hearts of our people as they express themselves.

What does the racial makeup of your team say about your church's value of racial diversity?

What atmosphere are you creating in your worship services for your congregation? Are you allowing and even encouraging different cultural worship expressions?

What is heard. What people see when they walk through the doors of your church is critical. However, what is *heard* is just as important. This is one of the most difficult tasks for the multicultural church. People are particular about their music. I have heard many stories about churches that have split over styles of music: the music is too loud or too soft; it's too funky or too chilled out; not enough or too many hymns are sung; too many new songs or too much contemporary music is played. It never ends.

Today, it seems some churches are resigned to have two or three "separate but equal" worship services. This way people can pick a traditional or contemporary worship service. Can you imagine people having worship wars in Jesus' time?

Though this is sad, it's an important issue we must address in a multicultural setting. In order for a multicultural worship ministry to have an impact, we must consider how people experience worship through music. People of different cultures often experience or respond to music in different ways. Some people assume that people of color respond to an R&B or Gospel sound while others respond more to acoustic or rock music. I have found that it goes all across the board and many times it is hard to predict. So, we try to incorporate all we can into our multicultural worship setting. Why not try to hit as many cultures as you can or even try to develop something new—something that we call a "third culture sound."

Key 1: Find your own worship sound (a third culture sound). If we are not careful, we can be seduced by what we hear on the radio and what the CCM Billboard says great worship music is. We long to re-create the latest Chris Tomlin or Tye Tribbett song. If only our worship team could do that song like David Crowder or Byron Cage. Our philosophy at Bridgeway has been to use those things only as a guide to our worship. Sure, we do a lot of familiar songs that are heard on the radio, but once we get together to rehearse, we play and sing the song as *we* do it, not the person on the recording.

We may do a song two weeks in a row. However, the song may sound a little different both weeks. Why? Because each week we rotate band members and singers. Those playing that week determine how the song sounds. And as the leader, I'm completely okay with that. I cannot tell you how many times I have told my band to play it the way *they* would play it, and my singers to sing it the way *they* would sing it. This creates freedom that allows the musicians to creatively explore the gifts God gave them. A multicultural congregation needs to develop its own sound, because what we hear on the radio is often created with a unicultural audience in mind. Let's create something new!

One of the most incredible things about doing ministry in a multicultural environment is that we get to experience things through the experience of someone racially different than ourselves. If you have been in a band or have sung with a team, you know this to be true.

Ronald Greene, Bridgeway's incredible band leader, is one of the most talented musicians I have met, and he has the spirit and humility to match. He is a gift to our worship ministry. When we were looking for a band leader at the church, I knew that we needed to hire someone who could play just about any style of music and would be open to creating a unique sound for our ministry. We brought Ronald on staff for that very reason (there were many other reasons, of course). When we rehearse, Ronald can turn any song into something that is distinctively "Bridgeway."

Ronald is a young African American man whose experience

has been in mostly traditional black churches. He is a great fit to our band because most of the others in the band have a rock/acoustic background. The sound is hard to explain. It is our third culture sound. You can't really call it a white, black, Asian or Hispanic sound. It's Bridgeway. It's the sound that rises from the musicians and singers of our congregation. It sounds like "us." That is the only way to describe it.

Key 2: Understand the worship leader's role in maintaining cultural balance in the music. It is the worship leader's responsibility to protect and maintain the cultural balance in the musical worship experience of your congregation. Nine times out of ten the worship leader chooses the worship music for the Sunday services. It is critical that we keep our pulse on the cultural dynamics of our congregation and provide the appropriate balance. The following are some practical ways to keep cultural balance in your worship experience.

- Diversify your playlist. We all have music that we love to listen to that aid our private worship moments. If we are not careful, we can create a whole list of congregational songs that we like. Sometimes this means our worship set may reflect one specific culture. This can derail our efforts to keep our worship experience multicultural. When you are listening to worship music for your Sunday morning services, make sure you choose music from artists of different racial and cultural backgrounds, or write your own.

- Find musicians and singers in your ministry that are capable of playing and singing different styles of music. This is critically important. If your music teams listen to one type of music, challenge them to go to the next level by listening to something different. Teach them how to explore new ways of playing and singing.

- Maintain a culturally diverse circle of friends and ministry partners. When our close circle of friends are racially and culturally diverse, we have a community of people that we can learn from and continue to bounce ideas off of.

Is the worship ministry at my church attempting to create a third culture sound? If so, how? If not, what can I do to encourage it?

In what ways am I, as the worship leader, maintaining cultural balance?

CULTURAL DYNAMICS IN MINISTRY STRUCTURE

When in a multicultural setting, we must always see our ministry and the structures we create through the lens of diversity. Countless resources are currently available for structuring music ministry. While most of them have beneficial content, they often do not work in diverse ministry settings. When we minister in a multicultural setting, it is important to be aware of the cultural dynamics of our team and how they may perceive the established structures and procedures of the ministry.

Based on their own experiences and quite possibly even through the lens of race, the people of your multicultural worship ministry will have different interpretations of the structure you set up. Elements such as whether or not to create an audition process, how information is communicated and disseminated, what takes place during your rehearsals, and how you choose music will need to be seen through the lens of diversity.

For example, for years at Bridgeway, we would have discussions about ministry auditions and whether to use them to get the right people to serve in the ministry. If you have been in music minis-try, you will surely understand the emotions that a topic like this can bring up in a church setting. Our ministry was open to any-one that had the desire to sing or play. The philosophy was pure and wonderful. The leaders at the time really wanted the people of our church to feel as though they easily could be a part of our ministry and find community.

Over time, however, we found that not having auditions was actually hurting our racial diversity in the ministry. The percep-tion of some was that there was no set structure by which to enter the ministry, and people from some cultures in our congregation were staying away from the ministry because of this issue. We've found that some people groups like more structure. They want to know that there is a defined way to do things, and they think in more linear terms. But some cultures tend to see structure as un-spiritual.

Keeping this in mind, we focused on two aspects in our audi-tion process. First, we developed a defined set of criteria in order to discern musical skill and gifting. And second, we did every-thing in our power to make the process extremely personal and relational. Being the leader of the ministry, I made sure that those who auditioned felt like they had time with me to talk about their lives, what they are passionate about and how they came to know Christ. This helped put people at ease about the process by com-municating that our ministry cared about them as people first and were not just interested in their musical gifts alone. I am con-vinced that our racial diversity increased due to our focus on these things.

We have been very intentional about how we structure the wor-ship ministry. We have made our audition process not only structured but also highly relational. Our rehearsal times are filled with laughter, work, tears and joyful singing. It seems as though people truly enjoy working and worshiping together.

WHY DO WE DO WHAT WE DO?

Ministry leaders in a multicultural setting frequently need to ask, why do we do what we do? Why do we struggle so hard to make multicultural ministry work? Why do we rack our brains trying to determine how something might be perceived from a cultural perspective? Why are we so concerned about things that seem so petty at times?

Because it is *worth it!* It is worth all of our effort because when we look at the congregation on Sunday morning and see the great diversity of God's people, we are pleased. And so is God.

Many suggest that cultural division doesn't exist among Christians. If that is the case, why aren't people of different races worshiping together? Why don't we see a beautiful mix of all God's people together on platforms? Why do we see a unicultural audience at Christian concerts? Perhaps your multicultural worship ministry could be used as a tool of racial healing in our world!

Maybe your ministry will change people's thinking about multicultural music and worship. Maybe God has brought your team of diverse people together to show an unbelieving world that God loves *all* people, and that together they can make an incredible sound for God's glory. This is what worship is meant to be. We pray, "Thy kingdom come, thy will be done on earth as it is in heaven." Do we mean it? If so, we need to examine what worship in heaven looks like. This is what the apostle John saw:

> I saw a vast crowd, too great to count, *from every nation and tribe and people and language,* standing in front of the throne

and before the Lamb. They were clothed in white robes and held palm branches in their hands. And they were shouting with a mighty shout,

"Salvation comes from our God who sits on the throne and from the Lamb!" (Revelation 7:9-10 NLT, emphasis added)

God is pleased when we do all we can to include all cultures in our worship gatherings. Just as we think through all of the cultural possibilities when welcoming people who don't know Christ into our gatherings, so we should ponder how to encourage people of all cultures to fellowship with us.

I am so grateful that when my husband and I walked into Bridgeway for the first time, someone thought about these issues so I would feel at home. Bridgeway is a place where I could thrive and be myself, where my cultural experiences and even my cultural hurts would be safe and I would find healing and a God who loves all people and wants them to be together, worshiping him. May the fullness of God be seen in your worship ministry as you continue to witness to his kingdom.

Mike's Story

A longtime friend invited Mike to Bridgeway. They grew up together in the same large Asian church. As Mike was now living in a place of hurt, he sought a church where he could be anonymous for a while. He did not seek out an intentionally multicultural church. But this is where he found himself.

"Even though I came to Bridgeway because I was running away from my old church, I kept coming back because I felt God ministering to me every time I went. It was in the sermons, the songs, the dramas and specifically the messages of Pastor Dan Taylor. And even though I didn't open up about what I was going through with a lot of people, I could tell people knew I was going through something and I could feel their love, too."

After some time away from his Asian church, he began to see how his Asian culture bled into the life of the church in both positive and negative ways. He felt great unspoken pressure to keep his problems to himself and try to fix them on his own. At Bridgeway, he found a place of grace that welcomed him and his problems with open arms.

Mike began playing guitar on the worship team and experienced another cultural difference between Bridgeway and his former church. The emphasis on excellence in the creative arts was new to him. He was not afraid of being thought of as "showing off" if he went for a solo or played "too loud." Nikki, the director of worship, impressed upon him this lesson: "God gave people talents to excel and hone those talents. If he gave one to you, then use it. If he gave you a talent and you're modest and hold back, are you using your talent as God intended?" This opened Mike up to a new level of freedom in his worship and expression of his other gifts.

While Mike did not specifically seek out a multicultural church, he found a place where people were intentionally made to feel welcome and loved no matter where they came from and were encouraged to bring their greatest pains as well as their greatest gifts to the body of Christ.

7 MULTICULTURAL PRAYER MINISTRY

Kwang Chul "KC" Whang

RECENT NATIONAL POLLS REVEAL THAT traditional Christian denominationalism is losing its grip. In a nutshell, that is the story of my potpourri Christian life.

Born in Seoul, Korea, I am a third-generation conservative Presbyterian. Or at least that was how it started. As long as I can remember, I attended church. My father was an official for the South Korean Ministry of Foreign Affairs. As a diplomat's kid, I had the privilege and challenge of living in many parts of the globe, experiencing a myriad of cultures and churches along the way.

In 1985 I married Dong Ok Hong, also a third generation Korean Christ follower, who is a charismatic, with conservative Presbyterian roots like me. Since our union God has shaped us over two decades with amazing experiences worshiping and ministering in a string of churches of various stripes, including Korean American Baptist, nondenominational charismatic, charismatic Episcopalian and Full Gospel African (Ghanaian).

In 2002 I landed at Bridgeway Community Church, where my forty-plus years of experiences coalesce comfortably under one roof. And based on many intimate conversations with Bridgeway brothers and sisters, my comfort in this gumbo soup of denominational and cultural diversity appears to be a fairly typical experience.

As an elder at Bridgeway, it is one of my greatest privileges and responsibilities to pray for the church and shepherd the prayer ministry. Based on what God has shown me through his Word and the many diverse experiences he's given me, I will share what I have learned about prayer in a multicultural environment. Prayer is a foundation for everything we do at Bridgeway and is a ministry in and of itself.

Prayer

The prayer life of a Christ follower should be as diverse and wide-ranging as daily conversations shared with family and friends. Unfortunately, in the greater body of Christ, prayer is often mistaken, misguided and reduced to a battle of formats. This is a risk in a multicultural church environment. People from different church traditions may view one form of prayer to be more acceptable to God than another, and try to force that form on the rest of the body or look down on others for praying a different way. At Bridgeway we have come to understand that prayer is not about the pedigree of its cultural or denominational origin, but the motive behind the words. The Bible has examples of prayer with drastically different styles and formats. They range from the poetic to the simple and direct. Yet God heard and responded to all of these petitions. This clearly demonstrates that prayer is a matter of the heart and not the form.

For this reason we must cease judging the ways Christians from differing backgrounds pray. We can enjoy, declare, participate, receive and celebrate the many forms of prayer in a myriad of tongues, all with the assurance that when we do so in accordance with Scripture, in the name of Jesus, God will hear our prayers. At Bridgeway we embrace this concept by encouraging all kinds of prayer (within biblical parameters) to bless our body. We have been blessed to tears by the simple prayer of an autistic child, a fiery spiritual charge by a Pentecostal brother, the babbling and rambling of a baby Christian, a heart cry of a Korean charismatic, a prayer in Hebrew by a Messianic Jew, and so forth. When we open our hearts and minds to accept the diversity of prayer traditions we have around us, we find ourselves blessed in so many different ways and discover new and rich ways to communicate with our Lord in prayer.

A MULTICULTURAL PRAYER MINISTRY

Bridgeway is neither the first nor will be the last to experience the blessings of a multicultural prayer gathering. We read in Acts 2 about a multicultural gathering of Jews from all over the world, where God poured out his spirit and three thousand accepted Christ in one day. Even in recent days we have witnessed many great prayer gatherings that cross denominational and cultural lines. Consequently, we dare not claim authorship or monopoly over this blessing. I believe that this blessing is available to all who embrace it.

The vision for a prayer ministry at Bridgeway was not designed or planned under the constraints and goals of creating a *multicultural* prayer venue. The multicultural aspect of this body was already part of our corporate DNA. The goal of those leading and championing prayer at Bridgeway is to make it *a house of prayer for all nations.* We want prayer to be ubiquitous at all levels of ministry and at all church venues. As a church we have much room to grow in this area, but clearly we are benefiting in countless blessings from the multicultural and multidenominational constituency of our church in Bible-ordained prayer.

The blessings we enjoy are not a simple joyride. With blessings come responsibilities. In order to cultivate a rich harvest at our multicultural prayer venues, the leadership has to be mindful of their flock-leading responsibilities and the mission of the church, which is *to be a multicultural army of God*. The leaders have to keep one ear open to the workings, leadings and promptings of the Holy Spirit while shepherding God's people from all walks of life and levels of spiritual maturity. Certainly, this is no easy task. It can be a hazardous walk in a minefield of misunderstandings. However, the rewards are great indeed. Every time I have the privilege of witnessing a victorious prayer event, I feel I have seen and tasted a slice of heaven.

Prayer Ministries

There are four foundational prayer venues currently operating in our church: Altar Prayer Team, elders prayer, Tuesday night prayer, and the fasting and prayer retreat. I wish I could paint a picture that would enable you to catch the essence of what we experience at Bridgeway. However, many of the concepts we discuss in this book are better understood and caught through experience and exposure than through academic teaching.

Altar Prayer Team. The Altar Prayer Team consists of teams available to intercede for those who come to the altar during and after services for one-on-one prayer. This group has another profoundly important task of gathering in the prayer room to intercede for the services while service is in progress.

The men and women who serve on our four rotating teams are all over the map in terms of prayer style. As best as possible, these teams intentionally consist of members that reflect the diversity of the church body in age, sex and race. The requirement to serve in this ministry is a deep commitment to a life of prayer, including intercessory prayer. In formulating the teams, we try to assemble a diverse group of prayer warriors so that those who come for prayer can exercise some discretion as to whom they pray with. For example, a man may be more inclined to pray with a brother over matters that may be better shared in the company of other men. We believe that the Holy Spirit will guide each person to just the right intercessor. We hope that making this option available lowers the threshold of resistance to those needing prayer.

Nevertheless, in practice, and contrary to our expectations, over time everyone on the teams experience the joy and privilege of praying with a variety of God's people. I am certain that even for some seasoned prayer servants on the team, this ministry provided their first opportunity to pray with people of different races and cultures. But the important thing is not that they pray with someone different than themselves but that God hears and answers their prayers. Hence, after some time, prayer ministers stop thinking about who they are praying with and simply focus on what the needs are before the altar. We have countless testimonies of Holy Spirit–led divine appointments, in which people were paired for prayer in simply amazing and miraculous ways, irrespective of race, culture or gender.

Elders prayer. The elders of the church meet together every week at 6 a.m. on Thursdays to humble themselves before the Lord, discuss matters of the church, pray for the church and uphold one another in prayer and accountability. This prayer-focused gathering profoundly influences the character, atmosphere and direction of the body.

Diversity is reflected among the elders in ethnicity (African American, Caucasian and Asian), leadership style (pastor, corporate CEO, retired teacher and businessmen), Christian heritage and experience, and prayer styles. However, these men fall on their knees in prayer, united at the foot of the cross, which dissolves the obvious disparities that can so easily create division. The miraculous spirit of unity that flows down from this prayer venue strengthens our church in so many ways.

Tuesday night prayer. The congregation is invited to gather together for a time of prayer each Tuesday night. Our senior pastor calls this venue the "secret weapon" of our church. No two evenings have been alike. There is no set agenda for the evening. The goal is to be Spirit-led. We have a general framework, but the rest is open to the leading of the Holy Spirit as needs become evident during the time of prayer and testimonies.

Typically, we gather at 7 p.m. on Tuesday night and take a few minutes for informal fellowship. The evening moves on to an opening prayer or song followed by a time of testimonies. Next, the leader, usually our senior pastor, shares a brief word or a teaching, and then leads the group in a time of deeply engaged corporate or small group prayer. We conclude the evening at 9 p.m. by having the participants touch and pray over every chair, door, aisle and hallway of the sanctuary in preparation for the upcoming Sunday worship and the harvest of souls to come.

The evening ends with the participants encircling the sanctuary, joining hands and concluding with a benediction. During this circle time the visual impact of the beauty and power of united diversity is displayed in its full splendor. As we look around the circle, we cannot help but be affected by the powerful display of spiritual unity. The unlikely sight of whites, blacks, Latinos, Jews and Asians holding hands with heads bowed and declaring "amen" in unison is a beautiful sight to behold. We can almost sense the delight of our Father in heaven.

During the evening, cultural diversity manifests itself in everything from the various accents heard in the prayers to the levels of intensity and forms of prayers. No one ethnic or denominational group has a monopoly over illness or financial or marital crisis. Regardless of our backgrounds, we all exist in this fallen world and battle the same earthly struggles. We unite against a common adversary by launching a spiritual counterattack with all kinds of prayer. As a result we have been privileged to witness many amazing testimonies and works of God unfold before us.

Genuine, passionate and seasoned prayer is infectious. Each of us learns from those who obviously have deep prayer lives. This venue has become a subliminal discipleship tool for our church. Without being overtly taught, our people learn how to pray. Additionally, we are exposed to a spectrum of prayer, not only affirming that there is no one way to pray but also experiencing prayer styles that possibly address our personal needs.

One particular Tuesday night prayer is indelibly etched in my soul. I, a middle-aged Korean man, got divinely paired up to pray with a mentally handicapped African American teenager. Justin was an obvious lover of Jesus. We shared our prayer needs and prayed for one another that night. I did not presume that because of my office of elder or my mental capacity that my prayers were any more effective than that of my young brother. I prayed fervently for Justin as best as I could, just as Justin prayed simply in his own way for me. I humbly received his prayer with a genuinely grateful heart. I was shocked to find out two days later, that Justin unexpectedly went home to be with the Lord the day after our prayer meeting. After his funeral I came to the realization that it was a tremendous privilege to have prayed with a young brother who received God's welcoming embrace before me! It was so poignant. Upon death and before God, it matters little who we are in the eyes of this world. God hears our prayers and loves us regardless of who we are. Irrespective of our backgrounds, it is only right that we pray for and with our brothers and sisters in Christ, for we are his creation and his beloved children, and he wants to hear from *all* of us without exceptions.

Fasting and prayer retreat. The men's fasting and prayer retreat is a regularly scheduled event held at Bridgeway Community Church. It is held approximately three times a year. Twenty-four hours are set aside over Friday and Saturday for the men of our body to come together in fasting and prayer. These gatherings have been life changing, unity building and powerful times of consecration.

The agenda for the event is framed around worship, testimonies, prayer and teaching. Prayer time is divided into individual, small and large group prayer sessions. We seal each retreat with communion and culminate the event in a time of fellowship and breaking of bread. The men's ministry organizers appoint leaders for various prayer sessions. A conscious effort is made to select worship leaders, prayer leaders and prayer groups to reflect the diversity in our church whenever possible. Additionally, care is made to understand the leaders' spiritual maturity and leadership skills.

The true beauty of this prayer event is that it unfolds supernaturally under a spirit of unity and orderliness in the midst of potentially chaotic diversity. We have witnessed this prayer event foster amazing crosscultural bonds of brotherhood among participants. Praying fervently and engaging in spiritual battle together opens a channel of love and respect for one another that defies social and cultural norms. When men—young and old, black, white and everything in between—humbly cast aside cultural, racial and denominational baggage, and unite to confront and bear down against the common enemy of our souls, an amazing transformation occurs. Men come alive as they become engaged in God's spiritual army.

Some of the greatest blessings that have resulted from these events are the strengthening of our men's ministry and the growth in the depth of the leadership of our church. The men of our church enjoy a unique blessing of fellowship that decimates stereotypical, cultural, racial and denominational barriers. The love that is shared among the brothers is genuine and evident. I often hear women remark how at our church, it appears the men have all the fun. Truth be told, it is simply the power of prayer at work at Bridgeway Community Church.

MAJOR FOCUS

Second Corinthians 3:17 declares, "Where the spirit of the Lord is, there is freedom." No matter how diverse the constituency of the prayer group, when we unite in the Spirit, worshiping and honoring God, the Holy Spirit approves and anoints the meeting and is free to reign. This unity, however, cannot be achieved without the key ingredient, love. Specifically, the love of Christ that we have received compels us to pray.

When the Holy Spirit is welcomed under the foundation of unity and grace-induced love, we experience God's blessing of freedom. This freedom is manifested in many forms and multicultural packages: freedom to express, freedom from chains of bondage, freedom from traditionalism, freedom to receive from God, freedom to love without the filter of skin color, ethnicity or religious heritage.

IMPLEMENTATION

We must keep *focused* on the lordship of Jesus Christ and conduct ourselves in love and humility while maintaining the unity of the Spirit in the meetings. The enemy would like nothing more than to create division and disunity among us by manipulating our differences. Understanding this tactic of the enemy, I believe that we must not only maintain but fight for unity. Leadership must be keenly aware of this.

This is spiritual battle. In order for unity in the Spirit to prevail in the heat of the battle, the leaders have to invest in prayer and fasting for the event. Thus prior to prayer events, our leaders get together, sometimes for a few days and sometimes for a week in advance, to fast and pray over the event. The return on this investment is so high I would never lead a prayer event without this level of preparation. This, I believe, is strategically critical.

Leaders must encourage participants to be *free* to worship and pray in any form: prostrate, seated or with hands lifted up to heaven. However, it is equally important to let the participants understand that they must share in the responsibility of being sensitive to the diverse constituency of the group and to keep all activities grounded in Scripture. I find that when each participant behaves with humble sincerity and honesty before God, there is little room for others to pass judgment on their behavior, no matter how unconventional the prayer posture may be.

We want to be *passionate* yet sensitive, and not bring offense or be offended by overt expressions of worship and prayer. Much akin to being free, we each have to be mindful that expressions made to God in public venues—whether the loudness or length of our prayers, a prayer language/tongue, or prophetic gifts—are not gauges of our spirituality, but gifts that God gave us to serve each other. I believe, according to the Word, that we serve a passionate God who prefers "hot or cold" but detests lukewarm relationships. Hence, passion is good, but unless it is genuine, it can open the doors to offenses given and taken.

Last, we do not gather in prayer to lord over each other because we are better or more spiritual than our brothers and sisters. We have to be mindful not to engage in counseling or correcting others through prayers. Such mistakes can be exacerbated in multicultural settings. Though possibly paved with the best of intentions, such behaviors can lead others to erroneously believe that the pray-er is displaying spiritual and cultural superiority. These unintended consequences can ultimately lead to quenching of the Spirit and endangering the environment of unity. When we gather to pray, we gather at the foot of the cross to humbly commune with God and to serve and support our brethren, *motivated* by the love of Christ alone.

CONCLUSION

Bridgeway Community Church is blessed to be in union and communion with Christ's followers that God has gathered literally from the ends of the earth. But for us to bask in this blessing, grace and love has to abound to cover a multitude of human deficiencies and sins. When brothers and sisters bring their diverse gifts of prayer to the buffet table we call Bridgeway and humbly serve one another under the lordship of Jesus Christ, motivated by

the love of Christ, we become participants in a beautiful, power-
fully liberating and passionate mosaic that is multicultural
prayer.

MULTICULTURAL CHILDREN'S MINISTRY

Karen Eastham

"WE DO NOT WANT TO PLAY WITH THE YUCKY people."

My friend had purchased a family of white dolls and black dolls for her daughters' dollhouse. One day, her neighbor's girls were home playing dolls with her children, and she overheard that statement from one of them regarding the family of black dolls. This was one of the eye-opening experiences that caused me to understand that we must have multicultural children's ministries. Children are so very spiritually open. If we want our kids to grow up knowing that *all* are precious in God's eyes, we must help all children understand that God did not make yucky people.

Researcher George Barna states that worldviews are formed by age thirteen; what we believe by this age we will likely die believing. As we get older, we build walls, filtering what we hear through what we believe to be true. As children we are most open to being instilled with an appreciation and celebration of the diversity that God created. We are commanded by Jesus to love one another as he loved us, and we must help our children to understand that those who accept Jesus as Lord and Savior are all brothers and sisters in Christ. We belong to one family.

BRIDGEKIDS AT BRIDGEWAY COMMUNITY CHURCH

Welcome to BridgeKids, the children's ministry of Bridgeway Community Church! I am the director of BridgeKids. I wish to share with you my personal journey of transforming our children's ministry into one that embraces, esteems and reflects *all* of God's children. I hope it will assist you in your quest to do the same.

I am a white woman who first came to Bridgeway as a seeker in June 1992. I was drawn to it from that first visit, largely because of the creative arts. I had never experienced a church so relevant and dynamic! I started attending regularly after finding out I was pregnant with my first child. I was not in the habit of going to church, but was convicted to raise my child in church. Sometime during my daughter's first year of life, I accepted Jesus as my Savior and Lord. I was an elementary school teacher, and I soon offered to take over the children's church to relieve the woman who had been doing it for the year the church had been in existence. At that time Bridgeway comprised about sixty adults and a handful of children. I have always found it amusing that God eventually called me to lead the ministry I was utilizing. I love his sense of humor!

As Bridgeway was growing and experiencing success in fulfilling the vision God gave David Anderson for a multicultural church, we began receiving many inquiries from other churches and secular organizations about *how* we did what we did. I vividly remember the day David told Bridgeway's leadership team that we each needed to be prepared to share with others what we knew.

I knew nothing! When it came to Columbia, Maryland, and Bridgeway, diversity seemed to be a norm. I guess I thought the multicultural nature of Bridgeway "just happened" as a result of the diversity of Columbia. I never realized the intentionality that went into it until I met with David to find out what I was supposed to tell people who asked me *how* we do what we do.

David shared with me that while Columbia was indeed diverse, the multicultural environment Bridgeway was located in was like the soil. The vision of being "a *multicultural* army of fully devoted followers" was the seed we planted in that soil. The four building blocks mentioned in David's opening chapter (see pp. 11-22) are the water and sun that God uses to help that seed grow.

That day I learned of the *intentionality* that went into Bridgeway. It was as if scales had been removed from my eyes! And with those eyes I looked upon Bridgeway's children's ministry, and it all of a sudden became clear to me how desperately I needed to "get intentional."

Maybe this is where you are right now and are wondering, *How do we get intentional?* Here are the building blocks of multicultural ministry as they apply to children's ministry.

PERSONAL CALLING AND COMMITMENT

I am so very grateful to God for using David to open my eyes to the fact that while I did indeed value diversity, I had been completely ignorant of the intentionality that is required to truly live it out and encourage it to thrive. To this day it is necessary for me to share this vision with my team, to assess where they are with regard to their own calling and commitment to it, and to dialogue regularly about how we will carry out this call in children's ministry.

Do you personally embrace the preciousness of all in God's sight?

Are you committed to living out the values of diversity in your church and in your children's ministry?

Do you know where your teammates stand with regard to this issue?

When was the last time you had a conversation about multicultural ministry with your team?

CLEAR VISION AND STAFFING FOR MULTICULTURAL MINISTRY

Vision. When I took that first look at Bridgeway's children's ministry with my new eyes, I realized how very white the ministry was. The kids we served were diverse, since the parents and guardians who brought them were diverse. But my leadership team, our music, our materials and our curriculum were white. So, we began by revisiting the vision, mission and values of our children's ministry, as well as our name.

Consider your ministry team and the people you serve. Is the area in which you live and serve diverse? (To determine this, ask yourself who gathers at the local Walmart.)

Does your church currently reflect that diversity?

Regardless of the answer to the previous question, does your team reflect that diversity?

Early on in my leadership of the ministry, I was introduced to a very successful children's ministry in the Midwest. There, I received a vision for what an effective children's ministry looked like. I even loved their name and "borrowed" it for Bridgeway. But now, with a desire to fully embrace multicultural ministry, I realized we needed to change the name of our children's ministry to one that celebrated who we were as a body. Thus Bridgeway's children's ministry became "BridgeKids."

Our new vision statement reflects our desire "to be a diverse community of maturing believers, equipping the next generation to embrace the ministry of reconciliation given to us by God in 1 Corinthians 5:18-20." This one closely aligns with our church's vision "to be a multicultural army of fully devoted followers of Christ moving forward in unity and love to reach our community, our culture and our world for Jesus Christ."

Our new mission became "building bridges to ALL people in Jesus' name," which mirrors our church mission "to build into each other as we build bridges to our community."

Our values remained the same as the children's ministry in the Midwest, with the addition of one, "Diverse." As only God could arrange, they were able to spell out the acronym BKIDS:

Bible-based (2 Timothy 3:16)
Kid-friendly (Matthew 19:14)
Intentionally relational (John 13:34)
Diverse (Matthew 28:19)
Safe (John 10:11)

When we had first decided on our values in 1995–1996, we intentionally decided *not* to include diversity or racial reconciliation, since we knew we valued these things as a church body. With my eyes now opened to how white our children's ministry was, I realized how desperately we needed to focus on truly living out multicultural ministry, so we added it as a value.

Consider the vision, mission, values and name of *your* children's ministry. Do they reflect your desire for and commitment to multicultural ministry?

What needs to be changed?

Take some time to pray and reflect on God's desires for your ministry.

Staffing. In 1999 my leadership team was mostly white and very female. It was composed of seven people: one African American and six Caucasians (one male). That July, we began discussing how to recruit more diversity onto our leadership team. We asked questions like, What should we be doing to be more culturally sensitive? Is there anything we're doing in recruitment that communicates a "white way" of doing and thinking? What can and should we do to attract more diversity? We discovered something our senior pastor already knew—the answer lies in relationships. Our sole African American team member was attracted to the team by the relationships she had built with several people on the team. We decided to be more intentional in building culturally diverse relationships. By 2001 our children's ministry leadership team was made up of six people: two African Americans, one Latino and three Caucasians.

Keeping a diverse leadership team is a constant challenge. My current team is comprised of six people: one African American and five Caucasians (all women). This team is phenomenal. And it is clear God has brought us together for this season. But I do look forward to future opportunities to once again build a culturally diverse team.

What does your staff look like? Do they all look like you?

Are you in relationships with a culturally diverse group of people? If not, ask God to show you who you can begin building relationships with.

When you have an opening on your staff, do you seek candidates who would bring diversity to your team?

Do you ask God to bring you the candidate who would bring the diversity you need? Are you willing to wait on the Lord to bring that person?

INTENTIONAL PURSUIT OF MULTICULTURAL MINISTRY AND RACIAL RECONCILIATION

Staging. As David said in the opening chapter, when people walk through the doors of our churches, they must see others that look like themselves, or they may feel out of place, like an outsider. We want the opposite to be true. We want them to know that there is indeed a place for them in our church. We want them to feel at home. In children's ministry this means that those greeting our families as they arrive and signing the children into their rooms should be diverse. Those serving in the rooms with the kids, shepherding, caring for and discipling them, should be diverse. Those leading them in worship and bringing them a word from the Bible should be diverse. This takes intentionality. We strive to ensure that people are serving in their area of giftedness and calling. As we do so, we must also consider how diverse each serving team is. Currently, BridgeKids's teams are balanced racially with Caucasians and African Americans. We need to recruit more Asians and Latinos.

At some point in our church's history, we were intentionally trying to grow our Asian population. One of our elders, an Asian, created a focus group of some Asians who attended Bridgeway to find out what were culturally relevant ways to attract Asians to the church and to participate in ministry. One of the things we gleaned from this gathering is that Asians tend to need to be asked personally in order to become involved. As a direct result, I asked that elder's wife to introduce me to Asians she thought might be interested in serving in our children's ministry. I arranged to meet personally with each of them. During these meetings, I invited each one to join our children's ministry team. Nearly all of them did! This confirms the truth that intentionally building culturally diverse relationships is the key to recruiting diverse leadership and serving teams.

What is the current composition of your ministry's serving teams?

Who do you need to be reaching out to and building relationships with in order to personally invite them to join your ministry?

Another issue we struggle with in the arena of staging is balancing our kids' ministries culturally. We have numerous programs where preschool and elementary kids learn how to use their various artistic gifts and passions for the glory of God. Most of these groups are composed of African American children. Some of these groups regularly minister to our congregation. As a part of intentional staging, we need to consider how diverse these groups are (or are not). I recently met with the leaders of each of these groups to be sure they were aware of the lack of diversity in their ministries, and to remind them of how critical intentionality is in the area of staging with regard to the continued pursuit of multicultural ministry and racial reconciliation. The next step is for each of these leaders to develop a plan for actively inviting children from other ethnic groups to participate in their ministry.

Materials. As we began this journey of intentionally pursuing multicultural ministry, I was horrified to discover how white our materials were in children's ministry. The Bibles we had on hand (for babies, toddlers and preschoolers) had no people of color in their illustrations, even though we knew the people of the Bible were people of color. Most of the other books we had on hand for kids during activity times also lacked people of color. The games we had available for kids to play did not display people of color on their boxes. Many of our toys (like baby dolls, dollhouse people and action figures) lacked diversity. The video clips we used from movies or television shows were white. The music we were using for worship was children's worship from a predominantly white church.

This was largely due to our ignorance of the need to be intentional in our selection of the materials. But once we became intentional, we discovered it was also due to a lack of diversity in the materials available to us. Things have significantly improved over the years, but I have yet to find a children's Bible that accurately illustrates the people portrayed in them. This continues to vex me.

My main advice is simply to be aware. Take a look at everything you use. Evaluate how diverse it is. Replace whatever is lacking. Make all new purchases and acquisitions with the intention to be diverse.

There are two other areas of concern. First is the use of promotional materials. As you create fliers, brochures and websites to market your ministry or an event, be sure the photos used portray diversity. Even if your church body is currently largely one color, portray what you want your body to look like. Second is the use of images of Christ. We tend to be very careful here. One of the best images of Christ I've ever seen portrays a multicolored face. None of us knows what he looked like when he walked this earth, but we can be fairly sure that he was not porcelain white with blue eyes.

Curriculum. When I first assessed the diversity of Bridgeway's children's ministry, we were using a curriculum purchased from a predominantly white church. This curriculum was wonderful and served us well for many years. Over the past two years we transitioned to writing our own curriculum. (We still purchase curriculum as the basis for our fourth and fifth graders.) There is nothing wrong with using purchased curricula. There are many amazing resources available. But please remember to look at the lessons and materials through the lens of diversity. Whether you purchase curriculum or write your own, always consider how culturally sensitive your lessons are.

For example, a particular curriculum we were using for kindergarten and first grade had an amazing series on "busting sin." When the kids came to large group time for a creative presentation of the Bible truth for the day, the set was a "sin-busters clubhouse." Each week, a different sin was busted.

One week, the sin being busted was lying. The kids were told a series of lies and asked to rate the lies on a scale of 1-10, 1 being a little *white* lie and 10 being a whopper of a lie. Then, the large group teacher turned the measuring stick over and brought out a second yardstick. The measuring stick used to rate the lies was all black and represented all lies. The other yardstick was all white and represented truth. Great point! All lies are equally sinful in God's eyes. You are either lying or telling the truth. Amazing lesson! Creatively done! Yet in ignorance, black was portrayed as bad and white as good. This is common in our society, but unacceptable.

A second challenge we have faced, whether using purchased curricula or supplementing whatever we were using with other resources, is a lack of diversity in video elements. We can't use most of the amazing resources because the casts are largely, if not completely, white. Thankfully we have the ability to make our own videos and have chosen to do so.

> Reflect on the materials you use or produce. Are they diverse? If not, what can you do to improve this?
>
> If you currently have great materials that do not reflect diversity, are you willing to change what you use in order to lift up this value?

ONGOING CONVERSATIONS ABOUT MULTICULTURAL MINISTRY

As David stated in the opening chapter, at Bridgeway we must continually talk about the value of diversity and how to ensure it is being fully lived out.

One such conversation I had with my team centered on our desire to get some time during the worship services to market our need for summer volunteers. We had tried something new the previous summer that had been quite successful and were planning to repeat it. We decided to use the testimonies of people who had served the previous summer and had enjoyed it so much that they became part of the regular children's ministry. I took advantage of this discussion to remind my staff how critical it is for us to remain intentional about recruiting diversity to our team, and that we needed to select men and women of varying ages and from various cultures to give their testimonies.

Another conversation had to do with our upcoming Palm Sunday services, where our kids would be ministering to the congregation through choir, dance and drama. We noted the current lack of diversity in these groups and had a lively discussion about it. We need to ensure that the children's ministry does not return to the one-culture state it was in when we began this process.

CONCLUSION

In Mark 10:14-15, Jesus said, "Let the little children come to me, and do not hinder them, for the kingdom of God belongs to such as these. I tell you the truth, anyone who will not receive the kingdom of God like a little child will never enter it." Children are so very spiritually open, they soak up the truth. What is the truth? That God desires that none should perish but that everyone would come to repentance (2 Peter 3:9). That others will know we are Jesus' disciples by our love for one another (John 13:35).

> Train a child in the way he should go,
>   and when he is old he will not turn from it.
>   (Proverbs 22:6)

We must instill in our children an appreciation and celebration of the diversity God created. Spend time in prayer asking God to reveal the degree to which your children's ministry embraces, esteems and reflects the preciousness of all in God's sight. Ask him how to ensure that the children entrusted to you and your team are fully equipped to fulfill the Great Commission: "Go and make disciples of *all* nations" (Matthew 28:19).

June and Larry's Story

When June and Larry first visited Bridgeway, they were pleased to find that their then four-year-old son, Jordan, was able to attend BridgeKids during the worship service. This was new to them, as Jordan had always joined them during the service after Sunday school. June and Larry were able to focus on worship and the message and see what Bridgeway was all about.

June and Larry were not looking for a multicultural church when they visited Bridgeway. They both came from traditional black church backgrounds. June believes this played an important role in making them who they are. "The [black church] has played a pivotal role in the black community for advancement, educational assistance and civil rights in addition to spiritual leadership and growth." They were not looking to leave their church, but as they moved farther from the city, it became more difficult for them to remain as active and involved as they desired. June remembers, "We began begrudgingly to find a new environment for our family."

They visited many churches, none of which were a good fit. One day a family member invited them to Bridgeway, saying, "It's different, but try it." So they did. It was indeed different. Larry liked it, but June still had some questions. When they picked up Jordan from BridgeKids, they were surprised to hear him say, "Can we come back here? I had fun." June and Larry looked at each other and realized they should come back because Jordan was captivated.

It has been nine years, and they are all still captivated. Larry serves in the Creative Arts Ministry attending to lighting during Sunday services and other church events.

June serves in BridgeKids and Women's Ministry. Reflecting on their whole church experience, June observed that prior to coming to Bridgeway, Sunday was their only day in a unicultural environment. Their workplaces and neighborhoods were all multicultural. When they gathered for worship in their black church, it was a time when they felt like they could be with people who looked like them as a family. She joked, "We didn't have to be on our best behavior." After being at Bridgeway for almost ten years, her perception of church family has changed, and she feels liberated in a different kind of way. Living and working in multicultural environments now extends to their Sunday worship.

9

MULTICULTURAL
STUDENT MINISTRY

Jared Sorber

TEENAGERS TODAY ARE SKEPTICAL OF THE
church and quick to point out its inconsistencies. They are looking for the real deal. They want to belong to a place that provides
an opportunity to be a part of something bigger than themselves.
I believe this is what student ministry at Bridgeway is becoming.
As students look around for answers and seek spirituality, we provide an environment that embraces them wherever they are. Our
ministries offer an opportunity to connect students with each
other and the gospel in a way that unicultural ministries simply
cannot.

Teens in our area go to diverse schools, work diverse jobs, play
on diverse sports teams and go to malls that ooze diversity. If
these students go to a youth ministry that does not match the rest
of their world, there will be a disconnect. The gospel will not fit
with the rest of their life. Even though no one is verbalizing it,
students will read between the lines and pick up the message that
Christ unites only those of the similar backgrounds. This is not
the gospel.

The message of the gospel is that God so loves the world and everyone in it that he sent his Son to die for us. The church's task is to share this message of Christ's love with people of all cultures. Because we have and share his love with all, God is actively breaking down walls and building bridges through the student ministries at Bridgeway. We are one body (1 Corinthians 12:12-13).

What cultures are represented in your students' schools, workplaces and so on that are not represented in your student ministries? (The U.S. Census website has wonderful information.)

Why is having your student ministry become more diverse important to you?

What are some opportunities you could take advantage of that would help your student ministry understand the value of diversity?

What are some potential problems with introducing the value of diversity to your student ministry?

In the next several paragraphs I will explain how Bridgeway student ministries are uniquely designed to be multicultural and to address the disconnect created between young people and the church as a result of not addressing diverse needs. We will look at three areas: (1) how we function as a ministry, (2) the importance of a diverse staff, and (3) how we teach our students to value diversity in their daily lives. If diversity permeates your philosophy, staff and students, you are well on your way to being a youth ministry that truly connects with the youth cultures in your community.

THE MINISTRY

Bridgeway student ministries are passionate about developing students from a variety of cultures and backgrounds into one community of fully devoted followers of Christ. We try to keep it simple: we are motivated by our love for God and others. This love drives us to make disciples of all nations (Matthew 28:19). This is a multicultural calling not bound by color, culture, class or creed, and is the motivation for international missions. It calls us to care about people throughout the world. The amazing thing is how well this verse applies to America today. Most of us don't have to travel far to encounter the nations. They are at our doorstep. And we no longer have to travel to a large city to encounter people from different cultures; the suburbs and even rural areas are rapidly diversifying. Information from the census in 2000 shows that the percentage of minority peoples grew in every state except West Virginia.

Many outreach ideas are used to draw new students to a youth ministry focus on reaching students from one culture. But as we carry out this mission to make disciples at Bridgeway, God is creating something unique in our youth ministry: diversity. We constantly ask how we can make *everyone* know that this is a place they belong. We want to be a ministry that reflects the diversity of our community and the kingdom of God.

How do we express diversity in the programs and activities we run for middle school and high school students? As we seek to connect students to each other and God, what will make students of all cultures feel welcome here? Do our music, staff, videos and environments reflect the diverse audience we are seeking to reach? As we communicate the truth of God's Word and worship together in community, we are intentional about who our communicators are, how we worship and how we live in community. As we equip students to minister and be disciples who make disciples, we teach the importance of bridge building and reconciliation. When our students are reconciled to those around them, it's a great illustration of what the gospel of Christ can accomplish.

Diversity permeates the thinking and planning of all our ministry. It starts with our mission statement, our values and works its way through our programs.

> What is your student ministry's mission? (What do you exist to do?)
>
> What are your student ministry values? These may be clearly laid out, or they might be implicit values woven into the fabric of your ministry, whether intentional or not.
>
> Is diversity represented in your mission and values? If yes, how is it played out in your ministry? If no, how can you reform your mission and values to show that you value diversity?

If diversity is not foundational to what you do, it will show, and some cultures will be disconnected from the group.

THE STAFF

Our goal is that students not only see the value of multicultural ministry through our programs and mission and values statements but also from the lives of our student ministry's paid and volunteer staff. I hope they see that I embrace diversity in my friendships and interactions with a wide variety of people. As they look at my Facebook page and see friends of all cultures and colors, I hope they realize that I practice what I preach.

The core leadership of our student ministry team exemplifies how we value diversity. We not only love God and our students, we also love each other. I gladly call the members of this team my friends. Even if we did not minister together, we would be friends.

God has blessed me with people gifted in areas that I am not. Matt Grubb is a big white dude that has been my friend since college. He is an extrovert who loves to challenge students to be better and do more. Matt's main responsibility is with the high school students.

Audene Johnson has been my friend for over eight years now. She is the voice of wisdom on our team and brings a much-needed woman's perspective. Audene is an athletic and competitive African American woman whose main responsibility is with the middle school students.

Dante Sheppard, the youngest and by far the coolest member of our team, is an extremely gifted dancer and actor. I have known Dante for ten years now. He grew up at Bridgeway and was a student leader in my ministry. After spending a few years at school honing his acting skills, Dante returned to oversee the student creative arts ministry. Dante is proud of his Puerto Rican and African American roots.

The rest of our student ministry's staff is also quite diverse. Our current staff includes people of Asian, African, Caucasian and Hispanic descent. They are split into four teams, one for each member of our core leadership team. Matt leads the high school team, Audene leads the middle school team, Dante leads the creative team, and I lead the small group leaders. All our teams do their best to show the diversity of God's kingdom in what they do.

A team with such different personalities from different backgrounds would not work in many church settings. But God has designed us to work together for his glory, and I wouldn't have it any other way.

Staff training and modeling is key to developing an effective multicultural ministry. People who sign up to join our ministry come from diverse backgrounds and have a desire to serve God in a diverse community, but they do not always understand how to live and teach in a manner that enhances reconciliation. So I try to model and teach our leaders in four key areas.

How is diversity embraced and expressed in your life?

Does the diversity of your youth leaders match up to the diversity of the cultures you wish to reach?

What is the next step you can take to develop or enhance diversity in your student ministry leadership?

Is your staff in the same place that you are when it comes to multicultural ministry? If not, how can you encourage them to grow in this area?

STAFF TRAINING

To help our student ministry staff become effective in multicultural youth ministry, we provide training in several key areas. The first is the area of *relevancy*. What our leaders say and who they are must be relevant to our students. This does not mean that our leaders need to dress and act like the students to connect with them. But they do need to be informed about students. They need to be students of the youth culture and of individual students in our group so they can credibly speak and relate to our students.

Adult leaders sometimes feel the need to fit in with the students, but this is not what students are looking for. They're looking for adults who sincerely care for them: the kind of caring relationship where walls of age and race are broken down. Being relevant to students is not an issue of coolness but of care.

The second teaching point for our staff is *humility*. I communicate to our staff that they are not the experts who will teach students everything they need to know about God and life. They should seek to learn as much as they can from the students. Our students are full of wisdom and have taught me many things through the years. The staff needs to be humble and approach students as fellow learners. They should walk alongside and be a support to our students. When relationships are in a multicultural setting, humility can go a long way. Because of family history, past experience, prejudice and much more, people approach relationships with different races in a variety of ways. If our staff members approach new students, especially students of a different culture, with an attitude other than humility, they might end up doing more damage than good.

The third teaching point is *authenticity*. Our staff needs to be real with students. I encourage our staff to be natural and share their culture with the students as they learn about our students' cultures. Students can see through fakes, but they respect those who are honest with them. I have found that when I share with students who I really am, they are more open to sharing who they really are. Most of the time we are complete opposites in the kind of music we listen to, the activities we like and where we like to hang out, but that does not matter. Honest sharing creates mutual respect. I could say that hip hop is my favorite type of music and I love to dance, but the truth is that I like country music and I love to ski. After the laughter about country music dies down, I often have great conversations that lead to ministry opportunities that otherwise would have been missed. Be who you are. Share who you are.

The final area we seek to model and train our staff in is that of *creativity*. We often use humor to connect with the students across cultural lines and engage them in a topic. You need to be able to laugh at yourself. Rather than repeating what has been done before, I encourage our staff to connect with students in new ways that show we care about them as individuals. Last winter we had a retreat with the theme "Identity." To creatively communicate the message and to break down cultural barriers, we had a white and a black staff member serve as MCs (master of ceremonies). Every time they were in front of the students, they adopted a different identity. First they were nerds, then goths, then thugs and so on. It worked great. The students eagerly anticipated what these guys from different backgrounds would be dressed like next.

How can you help your staff learn more about other cultures?

How would you gauge your staff's humility? What can your staff do to serve and care for individual students (especially those of other cultures)?

Who are you? What do you like and dislike? Why?

You are a unique creation. How can you use this to reach students of other cultures?

What creative means can you use to build cultural bridges and break down racial stereotypes?

OUR STUDENTS

When we last surveyed, we found that about 25 percent of our students are African American, 15 percent are Caucasian and ten percent are Asian, African, Caribbean and Hispanic. Until we started surveying our students a few years back, I didn't realize that many of our students come from diverse families. Over 50 percent of our students are multiracial. Many have parents who are not from the same racial background, and some have grandparents that are not from the same racial background. As I read the results of the survey and looked around Bridgeway, I realized that many families who formerly could not find a church to belong to, because they were not a unicultural family, found a home at Bridgeway.

Our students love their cultures and are proud of their backgrounds. We do not teach color blindness as a way to deal with racial differences; instead we seek to celebrate and learn about each other's cultures. Though color blindness may seem like a step in the right direction, it teaches us to ignore the beauty that each culture possesses. We learn about and celebrate the beauty of each other's cultures. We don't ignore the differences but embrace them. Through the years I have eaten many foods from around the world, have learned greetings in at least four different languages, have mastered the game of kongki (Korean jacks) and the art of hip hop dance (not!). Through students sharing their culture with me, I can celebrate who they are and where they come from. I hope they also learn something from me. This type of openness and learning tears down stereotypes and helps us truly appreciate our differences and see one another in a new light.

As a result of having diverse friendships, our students have

become extremely accepting and welcoming. When we go on a
trip or retreat and have new students join us, it always amazes
me that within a few hours it feels like everyone is part of one
group. Recently, we were at an event and a youth pastor thanked
me for how welcoming my students were to his group. It has
become almost second nature to many of our students to embrace new people and new cultures. Our students really care
about who people are and embrace others without allowing
judgmental views to create walls that separate. These walls and
judgmental views keep so many teen groups from being united.
Sometimes when we are traveling we get funny looks. It has to
be crazy from an outsider's point of view to see so many students
of different cultures and backgrounds who enjoy each other's
friendship.

Over the past several years we have taken missions trips to
South Africa and Mexico. I have found that traveling with a
multicultural group has several advantages. First, I have noticed
that a multicultural missions team has the ability to break down
walls in a manner that a unicultural mission team can't. Other
groups I have traveled with have been of one color, and when we
walked down the street in another country we stood out as a one-
race group. In one of those missions trips, many insults were
hurled at us by the locals. But with a multicultural group, people
are curious about how we work with so many different races. In
South Africa we had the opportunity to minister to both white
and black South Africans. I believe this was made easier by the
fact that we had black and white students in our group. On a trip
to Mexico those in our group who spoke Spanish were a huge
asset. They allowed us to make connections through their common language.

How well do your students welcome new students? How do they welcome students different than them?

What can you do to teach your students to be more accepting and less judgmental?

How can you celebrate other cultures with your students?

PREPARATION FOR MULTICULTURAL MINISTRY

God prepares people for the ministry that he calls them to. This is certainly true of my multicultural ministry journey. But God often does not reveal what we are being prepared for ahead of time. The journey that God takes us on prepares us for the work he wants us to do. The experience and insight I gained throughout my life is now benefiting me as a multicultural minister. When God brought me to Bridgeway as a student ministry intern in the summer of 1999, God had already been preparing me for multicultural youth ministry. I am amazed when I look back and see the people God put in my life and the opportunities he allowed me to experience; these helped build a vision for multicultural ministry in my life.

Since my first summer at Bridgeway I am now more intentional about leaning how to do multicultural ministry. I am intentional about the relationships I have and the people I can learn from. I have gone to many people in our church and asked questions about multicultural ministry. I have observed how other ministries in our church conduct their programs. I have also networked with other youth pastors from churches of different cultures to learn about their ministry and cultures. Let me encourage you to ask questions at your church and visit youth ministries from other cultures. You will learn much, which will push you to grow as a multicultural youth minister.

As you review your life, what are some ways God may have prepared you for multicultural youth ministry?

What are some ways you can prepare today for multicultural youth ministry?

Who are some people you can sit under and learn from?

What are some experiences you could expose yourself to that would give you more insight into running a multicultural ministry?

Challenges of Multicultural Ministry

Even with the best preparation, planning and support, there are still some challenges that remain. Though these challenges are tough, multicultural ministry is always worth it. I believe from the time of the early church multicultural ministry has been the call of God. I have seen students look at Scripture through other cultures' eyes, see new things and grow in their faith. I have seen students graduate from our ministry with a multicultural Christian worldview that I know will serve them well in life. I have seen students that can no longer settle for the ordinary. They have experienced a piece of what heaven will be like ("every nation, tribe, people and language" [Revelation 7:9]) and won't settle for doing church the way we have in America for the last two hundred years.

Multicultural youth ministry certainly is not easy. It would be much easier to focus on one group of people and provide programs that fit them. I don't recommend multicultural youth ministry as a strategy to fast growth in youth ministry. Although the potential for growth is much greater, transitioning from a unicultural to multicultural ministry will probably cause numbers to go down at first.

Often I have students and parents come to me with a great opportunity to attend a conference or major event. As we think
about taking our students to such events, I carefully examine
these organizations' values. They don't have to be as diverse as
Bridgeway, but through their websites and promotional materials, I try to discover whether they value diversity in the body of
Christ. If they don't seem to value diversity, the answer is no; it
does not fit our vision and mission. For many students and parents this is hard to understand because though they are a part of
our student ministry, they differ as to how much they value multicultural ministry. Some value it highly and understand what it
takes to be a multicultural body. Others are a part of Bridgeway
for a variety of reasons unrelated to multicultural ministry. They
may have other values in mind when they present conference
ideas to me. So this presents a great opportunity to teach parents
and students about multicultural ministries and other values of
our church.

It is also challenging to help students who love our diverse
ministry extend grace to unicultural ministries. There have been
times at conferences when students come to me frustrated and
even angry that the worship services are not diverse. Having
grown up at Bridgeway, they simply cannot understand how this
conference would not take the needs of a diverse audience into
account. This presents a great opportunity to teach students to be
gracious and accepting. It also gives me a great opportunity to
teach about true worship that is not bound by culture. This is a
valuable lesson for teenagers to learn.

Today's youth ministries need to be diverse to connect to the
diverse youth culture that is fast becoming the norm across America. God is raising up visionary youth pastors and leaders who

desire to unify the church and bring together young people of all colors and cultures in the name of Christ.

What challenges face your youth ministry as it becomes multicultural?

What are some ways you could communicate the value of multicultural youth ministry to parents and students?

Multicultural youth ministry is a journey like no other. There are tough challenges, but it is very rewarding to see the beauty of the body of Christ functioning as one. With God's power we can bring worlds together and see the unity that Christ prayed for (John 17:20-22) and the early church exemplified (Acts 2:42-47).

You can make a difference. You can be a leader who does not settle for unicultural ministry, but overcomes the obstacles to affect lives for eternity.

Epic

Epic is an event created by the student ministry leaders of Bridgeway with the help of several youth pastors from New York and Pennsylvania who desired to have an intentionally multicultural youth event that would call students to live out their part in God's epic story. During Epic, students look at how God has used a variety of characters throughout the Old and New Testaments and see through these characters' stories how God is calling them to live. Students interact with the characters through discussions and interactive experiences including service projects. As students discuss the characters, themes like diversity, grace, forgiveness, reconciliation and love arise and challenge the students to examine their lives. Students also get a glimpse of what Bridgeway is like through the diversity expressed in worship, drama, dance, video and more. Epic is specifically designed for high school students who have a relationship with Christ and desire to grow into what God calls them to be.

After our first year of Epic in the summer of 2009, we have already seen students energized about carrying out the mission of God. Students left motivated to impact their world by being who God has called them to be. They impact others by being examples of Christ who broke down barriers and built bridges to those who needed him so badly. Students see that God has called the church, a diverse group of people left on earth to be God's hands and feet, to be the hope of the world.

Epic's Mission: to help students unfold their chapter in God's epic story

Epic's Vision: to create an experience where students can find their epic story in God's, and to live out their story each day

Epic's Values:

    Community: coming together to learn and live

    Diversity: reflecting God's whole body

    Creativity: expressing our God created uniqueness

    Relevancy: connecting to people where they're at

Epic takes place each summer in the Baltimore, Maryland/Washington, D.C., area. For more information on Epic go to www.EpicStory.org.

COMMUNITY OUTREACH

Dave Michener

WHEN I WAS A KID I ACTUALLY BRAGGED about my dad and my friends bragged about theirs. *"My* dad can hit a baseball as far as any man in the world!" "So? *My* dad is so smart that his boss promoted him at work, so now he makes more money than *your* dad!" "Well *my* dad can beat up *your* dad!" "Well, if *my* dad *let* your dad beat him up then *my* dad wouldn't even cry! So there!"

So which dad was actually better? Well, *my* dad, of course! Seriously. The answer really is *my* dad. All kidding aside, the reality is that God gave us each of us our dads for a reason. Some of us will never learn that reason this side of heaven. But nonetheless, I am hesitant to say that one dad is better than another. Like I said, I'm hesitant, but that won't keep me from saying it. I think my dad is the best in the whole wide world.

And at the risk of sounding arrogant, while I believe that God uses all kinds of churches for different seasons in life and different reasons of life, I believe that multicultural churches are the best churches ever. Once again, I'm not dismissing that God is working in many unicultural churches, but I have a sense that he smiles in a special way when he sees a multicultural church committed to reaching its community for Christ.

Bridgeway's vision is that we would become "a multicultural army of fully devoted followers of Christ moving forward in unity and love to reach our community, our culture and our world for Jesus Christ." Each one of these action words and descriptive words were chosen very carefully. We believe that being a multicultural church is essential for reaching our community, our culture and our world for Christ. Why? In this chapter I will build a case for the unique place of the multicultural church in community outreach. Here are four reasons multicultural churches have an advantage over unicultural churches when it comes to community outreach.

1. A multicultural church paints a perfect picture of the power of reconciliation—which is at the core of all community outreach.

> All this is from God, who reconciled us to himself through Christ *[the model]* and gave us *the ministry* of reconciliation: that God was reconciling the world to himself in Christ, not counting men's sins against them. And he has committed to us *the message* of reconciliation. We are therefore Christ's ambassadors *[the messengers]*, as though God were making his appeal through us. We implore you on Christ's behalf: Be reconciled to God *[the mission]*. (2 Corinthians 5:18-20, emphasis added)

The perfect relationship between Creator and creation was broken in the Garden of Eden when Adam sinned. He didn't realize it at the time, but when he broke the only rule God gave, he actually voted all of humankind off the island. The beautiful relationship needed repair. Our sin separates us from our just and holy God. God provided the solution, the healing agent, the satisfactory payment for the penalty of our sins through Jesus Christ—the unique, one-of-a-kind, perfect, God-man substitute. When Jesus died, he created a bridge between God and humans. This bridge allowed for the re-creation of relationship between God and humans. We are reconciled. Two parties once at odds could now be unified again. While Adam's sin had a corporate impact, it requires an individual response. This bridge must be crossed by each and every individual in order for them to be reconciled with God. Love received from God creates reconciliation between God and people. Reconciliation is at the heart of the gospel.

God chooses the church to be the living example of the reconciliation of God and people. Christ is indisputably the model of reconciliation. God commissions each Christ-follower to have a ministry of reconciliation. The centerpiece of that ministry is a message of reconciliation. And since every message needs a messenger, he sends us all on a mission to spread the word about reconciliation.

Without the church's example—people reconciled despite their differences, their histories, their hurts and pains, their uncommon experiences, their comparative gaps in education and economic resources—reconciliation to God seems like a pipe dream. But when an angry, hurt, divided, frustrated world looks at the church and sees forgiveness, love, unity, acceptance, appreciation and even celebration of differences, it is compelled to know more. With the picture of a reconciled multicultural church, God's love and power is authenticated.

Pastor John felt the same way as the apostle Paul about the power of love when he wrote:

Dear friends, let us love one another, for love comes from God. Everyone who loves has been born of God and knows God. Whoever does not love does not know God, because God is love. This is how God showed his love among us: He sent his one and only Son into the world that we might live through him. This is love: not that we loved God, but that he loved us and sent his Son as an atoning sacrifice for our sins. Dear friends, since God so loved us, we also ought to love one another. No one has ever seen God; but if we love one another, God lives in us and his love is made complete in us. (1 John 4:7-12)

Reconciliation between God and humans creates the potential for reconciliation between people of different cultures. Demonstration of love within the church lets people outside the church know that God is with that church. And love inside a church makes people love their church and prompts them to tell people on the outside.

Here's just one of many examples from real life that demonstrates how all these reconciliation "dots" can be connected. One of our community's high school principals, let's call him Malcolm, showed up at Bridgeway one day at the invitation of a co-worker. Malcolm is in a biracial marriage. He's black and his wife is white. Malcolm and his wife went to an all-white church for many years. It would probably be more accurate to say that Malcolm went to Christmas and Easter services for many years with his wife at her all-white church. Mrs. Malcolm went consistently every week. Malcolm went consistently twice a year.

But when his white assistant principal—let's call him Frank—who was his true-blue wingman at work, told him that Bridgeway was a multicultural church that used the creative arts to express the message of the Bible, Malcolm was intrigued. Malcolm loved the service. He thought the worship was kickin', the drama was funny and authentic, and the message from the Bible was practical, relevant and actually made sense. He greatly appreciated the attempt at excellence, and the use of media connected with him as he dabbled in the techie stuff as a hobby. But the thing that blew him away was the way people of all races interacted. He had never experienced or even heard of this happening in any setting where it was not required by a policy or employee handbook. Malcolm brought his wife with him the next week, and they began coming consistently, not just twice a year consistently, but the week-in and week-out kind of consistently.

He was so curious about the dynamic that he asked Frank and his buddy Rich if they could go out together to shoot some pool and talk about it. It didn't take long before Malcolm cut to the chase and asked Frank and Rich, "How do you guys *really* pull this multicultural thing off?" Rich shared some of the intentional things we do with our staging and our staffing, but the real answer was that Christ does the reconciling. Malcolm couldn't believe that that's all it was: Jesus! So he pushed even further. "C'mon, guys. You can tell me. It's just me—Malcolm. What's the *real* secret? People from different races, colors, classes and cultures don't want to be nice and spend time praying and playing together because of religious experience. Talk to me!" And with that he grabbed a napkin and a pen and prepared to take notes on the secret of multicultural unity.

Frank stuck to the script, explaining that reconciliation between people overflows from the reconciliation experienced between God and a person when that person trusts Christ alone for forgiveness of sins and eternal life. Because we are reconciled with God, we can be reconciled with each other. Christ creates unity. It's not a program or religious experience but a response to a personal relationship with Jesus. Sin separates, but Jesus unites. No smoke and mirrors. No dog and pony show. No secret code. Simply put, a relationship with Jesus transforms our relationships with others.

Malcolm was buying it because the Holy Spirit was selling it and Frank, Rich and hundreds of others at Bridgeway were living it. Malcolm trusted Christ personally because the powerful example he saw and experienced created a curiosity in him that he couldn't leave unresolved. So a black man from North Carolina, opened up to a white guy from West Virginia and a white guy from Chicago while shooting pool. The Bridgeway boys had the answer Malcolm was looking for. Malcolm not only trusted Christ but became a consistent servant at Bridgeway and an ambassador for reconciliation in the community for many years before his career took him back to North Carolina.

Study 2 Corinthians 5:18-21.

What are the implications for you as a leader?

How should this passage affect your church and its motivation for outreach?

By its very nature of restoring relationships, reconciliation demands that we be bridge builders. A bridge makes a total commitment to the other side, the other people. A bridge has a way of saying, "I'm coming to you. You are that important." A dock has a way of saying, "I'm over here. I'll come part way but you need to come to me. And at the end of our little visit, I will go back to my side of the shore where I'm comfortable." Are you a bridge builder or a dock builder?

What are some ways you can move from being a dock builder to being a bridge builder?

2. A multicultural church creates a curiosity in the community that can be leveraged for community outreach in a unique way.

The comedian Steve Martin used to do a bit that was strange but weirdly funny (to me anyway, although my parents never found humor in him). It would go like this: "I just want to meet a girl with a head on her shoulders. I hate necks. That way, when we go to a fancy restaurant and I walk in with her, every head turns. Except hers—she has no neck!"[1] (So, you don't find that funny either?)

If I were sitting in a restaurant and a neckless woman sat at the table next to me, I would be tempted to gaze at her.

What's the point? When we see something we've never seen before, we become very curious and want to check it out for ourselves. Especially if it seems unbelievable. So when a church, a place of worship, a community of faith intentionally builds bridges of reconciliation, it creates curiosity. People just have to see for themselves.

I can't tell you how many times I have been in our community with a group of Bridgeway friends and people stare at us. When people see a group made up of black, white, Asian and Latino folks laughing, sharing a meal, joking or serving the community together, they gawk!

When a multicultural outreach team serves at our Homeless Day Center, feeds the homeless who live in inner city Baltimore, delivers meals to homes at Thanksgiving and Christmas presents to children whose parents are incarcerated, those being served become curious. I call this *the curiosity quotient*. Multicultural congregations serving their community leads to a good reputation,

---

[1]From the comedy sketch "You Naive Americans," in Steve Martin, *A Wild and Crazy Guy* (Burbank, Calif.: Warner Brothers, 1978).

which leads to a curious community, which leads to spiritual conversations.

Curiosity leads to questions and conversations. And questions and conversations lead to stories of transformation and relationship with a God of grace and forgiveness. These God stories are powerful because they are authentic and based on the authority of the Bible. People are inclined to want that same peace and unity.

This curiosity is not just a channel God uses to introduce himself to people who do not know him personally. He also uses it to create desire for oneness in the body of Christ among Christians who have never experienced it in their relationships.

For Bridgeway's ten-year anniversary, we held a gala at a big hotel in downtown Baltimore. We pulled out all the stops. The hotel was luxurious. The food was exquisite. Everyone was dressed to the nines. And the program was all done in the spirit of the Grammy or Oscar awards ceremonies. Our hosts were a white guy, a Latino brother (both in tuxedos) and an African American sista (in a long gown). They were classy, professional and funny! *Really funny!* We had a multicultural music group and stellar band. We had inspirational greetings from a number of leaders within the church and from outside the church. It was a praise party like none I have ever experienced. And yes, it was indeed a party!

One of the speakers that night was Bill Hybels, senior pastor of Willow Creek Community Church in South Barrington, Illinois. When our senior pastor, David Anderson, was an intern at Willow under the leadership of Bill Hybels, he became inspired to not only plant a multicultural church but one that would use the creative arts to communicate the dangerous message of the gospel of Christ. Having Bill be with the Bridgeway people ten years after the birth of this dream was extra special to all. Bill had some very kind words of affirmation for us that night, but little did we know the impact we had on Bill.

At the Willow Creek Leadership Summit a few months later, we learned what the experience of that night meant to Bill and for the future of his church. As Bill stood before thousands of leaders, with passion and a quiver in his voice he said,

> We've taught more about reconciliation here at Willow in the last twelve to eighteen months than we have in the first twenty-five years. We've brought in teachers of diversity and worship leaders of diversity more in the last eighteen months than in the first twenty-five years. We've challenged ourselves to demonstrate racial diversity on our stage every midweek and weekend service. And most of the time, almost all of the time, we do that. We've done staff training on this and we're more and more committed to making our staff hires and elder-board additions people of diversity. And maybe this is the simplest way I can say it: We are bound and determined to become a multicultural congregation. And we believe that this will bring a smile to heaven. Now, I'm not trying to say that everybody is asleep at the switch on this. Many of your congregations are already this. Bridgeway Community Church out on the East Coast are way ahead of us. I spoke at their ten-year anniversary out there. It was probably one of the most holy moments I ever had, seeing the celebration—not the toleration—but the celebration of the diversity in the family of God. I'll remember that night the rest of my life. I want you to know my heart on this. We are moving down that track, never to give ground back.

At the Willow Creek Association Leadership Summit, I

watched an interview with rock star-turned-humanitarian Bono, of the band U2. When asked what makes him want to go to church, he replied, "I go where the life is. What I can't stand is a lifeless ceremony where there is no honesty and humility. I will go to a church that's a place where everybody's welcome regardless of what they look like or even how they act. I will feel comfortable there."

A multicultural congregation creates curiosity in the community that leads to spiritual conversations that God uses to reconcile a lost and dying world to himself. And a multicultural congregation creates curiosity in the church that inspires leaders to shape their churches in a way that shares the message of reconciliation through their everyday experiences.

Assess Your Reputation in the Community

Do you know what people of various cultures are saying about your church?

What is the word on the street about your church?

To find out you may consider joining a community board for a foundation or human services. You may want to be a regular at the Chamber of Commerce meet-and-greets. Invite unchurched friends and neighbors to your church and have them observe your Sunday service. Afterward, take them out for a meal and ask what they liked and disliked about the service. Ask them to describe the social climate of your church. Listen and learn.

Address the Info

What does the feedback tell you?

What are the implications?

What are some things you can do to strengthen your "curiosity quotient" in the community?

Apply the Strategy

Don't just talk. Try something different. After a few months of these intentional new initiatives in the community, continue to listen at the boards you serve on, at the Chamber meetings you attend, and to the unchurched friends you ask for honest feedback. Keep doing it. Don't underestimate the power of the "curiosity quotient" in the community. Good news spreads much slower than bad news, but it will still spread. Be patient.

3. A multicultural church conditions its congregation to build bridges to the community because it has already broken down barriers and built bridges across cultural lines within the church.

Every Tuesday night we have a little family reunion at Bridgeway. Though it's not so little anymore, it remains a fraction of our Bridgeway attendees. Our prayer gathering on Tuesday nights affords us the opportunity to be up close and personal with a smaller segment of the congregation. We have this really cool, catchy, intriguing name for this gathering: Tuesday Night Prayer. Pretty creative, huh?

There is a God-ordained phenomenon that takes place every Tuesday night in that crowded room. People of a variety of colors, classes and cultures actually have conversations with each other and with God. Are you impressed yet? Think about it before you write the concept off too quickly as overly elementary. People of different colors, classes, and cultures share their pain, pasts, pre-

dicaments, problems, praises and personal stuff. And they sometimes lay hands on each other while praying. That's right. They
touch each other.

Their cultural comfort zones get shattered by the power of the
Holy Spirit. When we challenge them to share their faith with
family and coworkers, they already have lots of practice stepping
beyond what they're used to, taking risks and talking with people
they thought they had nothing in common with. They have not
only survived but have seen God use them and touch them in
supernatural ways. What an evangelistic advantage this multicultural army has!

What cultural barriers exist in your congregation?

Why do they exist?

Have you talked about them at the leadership and the congregational levels?

Consider going back to the basics and emphasizing praying
together and serving together.

What would that look like for your church to be like the
church in Acts 2, which was devoted to God and each other?

*4. A multicultural church positions itself for exponential results in
evangelism because it is obeying God by simply being who they are.*

Bridgeway has over fifty cultures represented in our congregation. But we are not only multicultural, we are also multigenera-
tional. You might be surprised at the ease with which people from
all these cultures and generations interact. Bridgeway is truly one
congregation with multiple faces. We all have one common mission, one vision, one set of values, with slightly different methods

of delivery depending on age-appropriateness or seasons of life. But we are definitely one church. In the lobby after a Sunday service, at a men's breakfast, at a women's brunch or at a community service project, you will see people from all different cultures interacting, serving, playing, praising, laughing and crying together. This oneness across cultural lines is a direct answer to the high priestly prayer of Jesus recorded in John 17:20-23:

> I pray also for those who will believe in me through [the disciples'] message, that all of them may be one, Father, just as you are in me and I am in you. May they also be in us so that the world may believe that you have sent me. I have given them the glory that you gave me, that they may be one as we are one: I in them and you in me. May they be brought to complete unity to let the world know that you sent me and have loved them even as you have loved me.

Not only does oneness in a multicultural setting complete the prayer, it confirms to the world that Jesus is who he says he is: God! Complete unity brings confirmation.

Jesus instructs his followers to make disciples of all nations. This is a daunting task. Just think about how strategic it would be if our missionary teams, both local and global, consisted of people of all different cultures. The pool of volunteers in a multicultural church is already representative of the cultures present in the community. When outreach teams are naturally diverse, they are positioned to reach a wide variety of people groups.

The celebration of all cultures in the creation of a new Christ-centric culture is direct obedience to the teaching in James that demands culture and class favoritism be done away with in the church.

Obedience brings blessing (Deuteronomy 6; Galatians 6)!

Blessing comes in many different forms: one is seeing a plentiful harvest of fruit from the cultivating and planting of the gospel through our outreach efforts. A multicultural church stacks the deck for God, and it has a big payoff. Galatians 6:7 says we reap what we sow. It reminds us to never give up because payday is coming. A multicultural church positions itself in a unique way to see God bless in significant ways. It is an answer to Christ's prayer for unity; it confirms Christ's authenticity; it constructs a strategic vehicle for fulfilling the Great Commission; and it creates a cause and effect between obedience and blessing.

Do you believe the multicultural church has an advantage in reaching its community? Or at least do you recognize that a multicultural church can reach its community in ways that a unicultural church can't or at least would find very difficult?

> Make a list of all of your church's outreach initiatives. Then look at those initiatives and ask yourself, *If my church were truly multicultural, would this outreach initiative be weaker or stronger?* Then make another list of outreach initiatives you could start if you were a multicultural congregation. For those churches that are already multicultural, why not play to your multicultural strengths? What outreach initiatives could you launch in the near future?

Remember my bragging that my dad was better than all other dads? Some reasons for that are that I love my dad; I believe in my dad; I've had wonderful experiences with my dad; and my dad has proven himself to me. Well, I have a tendency to think that way about the multicultural church for the very same reasons. The multicultural church is uniquely positioned to reach its community.

I am not a salesperson, but when I get passionate about something (like I am about my dad), I really want to tell my friends. I have experienced the lifesaving and life-sustaining grace of Jesus. I want to tell people about him. Don't you? I've also experienced the immense joy and adventure of living, loving and leading in a multicultural church. I've not only seen the power of spiritual reconciliation but experienced the profound power of relational reconciliation—quite often around the issue of race. It is so amazing that I want you to experience it!

Not only is relational reconciliation awesome, it helps us reach our community. Let me summarize my case: (1) A multicultural church paints a perfect picture of the power of reconciliation—which is at the core of all community outreach. (2) A multicultural church creates curiosity in the community that can be leveraged for community outreach. (3) A multicultural church conditions its congregation to build bridges to the community because it's already breaking down barriers and building bridges across cultures in the church. (4) A multicultural church positions itself for exponential results in evangelism because it is obeying God simply by being who they are. The verdict may still be out, but I think I have a solid case.

11 GOING FURTHER

Margarita R. Cabellon

THERE YOU HAVE IT. That is the whole Bridgeway Community Church experience contained in a book. Well, almost.

We have talked about the importance of intentionality and staging in a multicultural context. We have newfound confidence in running safe and open conversations on race in a group setting. We have discovered a new expanded musical library that now includes genres spanning from gospel to contemporary Christian artists. We have seen how humor draws in teens and how important it is that an entire curriculum for children reflects people from different cultures. Now all we need to do is put our running shoes on and get started.

Too easy, right? Of course not. Anyone who has wrestled in the multicultural-ministry ring knows it is a lot harder than it looks or sounds. Embarking on the journey of intentional multicultural ministry is not easy. Our team has done its best to share the successes and failures of leading an effective multicultural church, and we hope that we have answered many of your questions and left you with some practical steps to apply to your church. We pray that the wisdom found in these pages continually encourages you to fight the good fight toward building the body of Christ that reflects how it will look in heaven—multicultural and beautiful!

If after reading this book you are interested in more hands-on help or instruction from our team, we are here to serve you through the BridgeLeader Network (BLN), the consulting arm of Bridgeway Community Church. BLN is a private, nonprofit 501(c)(3) organization established in 2000. Our mission is to *assist, inspire and develop organizations to increase multicultural effectiveness.* I am the current director of BLN. David Anderson and our team can meet with you, your staff or congregation depending on your particular ministry needs.

After almost ten years of ministry, BLN has developed numerous activities and training programs designed to assist organizations wherever they are on their respective journeys. In this chapter are some of those resources and how they have assisted real-life ministries and the communities they serve. If you think your ministry could benefit from any of these services or some other consulting help from us, email us at info@bridgeleader.com.

VISIT BRIDGEWAY

This is the simplest and best way to start the ball rolling. On Sunday mornings we welcome many pastors, church planters and seminary students who are eager to see if what they hear about our ministry actually plays out in real life. Call or e-mail BLN ahead of time to let us know which Sunday you plan to visit the church. BLN will arrange a tour of the church and the opportunity to meet with some of our ministry leaders and staff members. Again, wherever you are in your ministry, we welcome you to check us out. If you are too far to visit, our services are webcast live on Sunday mornings at 10:00 a.m. and 12:00 p.m. at www.bridgewayonline.org.

SPEECH OR SERMON

This is the most popular "starter" service that BLN offers. Dr. Anderson or a member of the BLN team will speak for up to one hour on concepts relating to multiculturalism, racial reconciliation and diversity. This is often set within the context of a Sunday worship service or leadership conference.

Here is a brief list of the most-requested topics:

- Five Behaviors of Multicultural Leadership
- The Rhythms of Reconciliation
- How to Have a Good Fight
- The Adversity of Diversity
- Moving Forward on the Racial Reconciliation Continuum
- Multicultural Evangelism as a Step Toward Multicultural Ministry
- Four Things I've Learned by Doing Multicultural Ministry
- Transitioning from a Unicultural to a Multicultural Ministry
- When the Call Comes (on leadership and discerning life's purpose)
- Picture Perfect (on unity, now and in the future)
- You've Got Issues (on personal change and guarding one's heart)

Pastors seeking to plant the vision of multicultural ministry in their existing congregations most often request this service. It's not unusual for pastors of a unicultural church to see the changing demographics of their surrounding community. Often these pastors desire to transition to multicultural ministry long before their congregation does. To start the conversation BLN has been called on to help cast this vision in these churches.

SEMINARS AND DOWNLOADS

Seminars and downloads come into play when the pastor or leader of an organization decides that it's time to start "doing" multicultural ministry by getting the rest of their leadership team on board. BLN will travel to teach concepts relating to multiculturalism, racial reconciliation and diversity to pastors and their ministry leaders in seminars that range from a few hours to one to two days long in your city. BLN can also provide a creative component using dramas, videos or dance to illustrate key messages regarding racial reconciliation and doing life with people across cultural and ethnic lines.

For example, BLN conducted one of these more in-depth consultations in March 2008 with a growing multicultural church in London, England. The pastors there conducted a six-week sermon series based on Dr. Anderson's book *Gracism: The Art of Inclusion*, and invited Dr. Anderson and his team to end the series in a large, multichurch weekend event. The impetus for this series was based on the changes the pastors saw in their community and within their church. For years, that church was a nondenominational, unicultural church housed in a hundred-year-old church building in southeast London. More and more immigrants, especially from Eastern Europe and Africa, were becoming regular attendees. Additionally, with the increased immigration came increased racial tensions in the surrounding community. Diversity had come and they had to choose between saying "Welcome" or "Welcome Home" to the new attendees.

BLN spent that weekend listening to the elders and other ministry leaders in the church to hear how the changing demographics affected them and the questions and struggles they had in adapting to these changes. Dr. Anderson also addressed the congregation (and leaders of about sixty other affiliated churches) three times about what it means to be a "gracist" in an ever-changing and sometimes hostile society. Participants shared both their joy and apprehension about crossing cultural lines. Just as in the United States, there are both overt and covert racial tensions that people are hesitant to address lest they say the wrong thing or be misunderstood. In the end we heard from the church staff and church members that they felt encouraged and more unified as a church body as a result of the "gracism" sermon series and weekend consultation. This is just one example of how BLN has taken the message of racial reconciliation and gracism to a church and community, providing practical and healing steps toward unity.

ROUNDTABLE DISCUSSIONS

If a whole download or weekend event is more than what you are seeking at the moment, a RoundTable Discussion is another option for creating a safe space for discussion in a shorter time period. At BLN we enjoy conversing about a potentially divisive topic, discussing and discovering what God's Word says about it. Christians in the West easily get comfortable in their Christian bubbles, never having to interact with people with different worldviews, from a different class or with different skin color and accents. In fact, Western Christians can simultaneously give to the poor without ever having to see the poor. We can fervently argue that racism and prejudice in all forms is sin, yet at the same time have no friends or acquaintances not of our ethnic background outside of the workplace.

Through conversation, BLN addresses these contradictions, not to condemn or judge but to discuss, in love, that the Christian faith is about the hearing and the doing of the God's Word. When

God says "love thy neighbor," he does not mean only the neighbor who lives in your cul-de-sac. He also means the people on the street we fear when we see them walking near our cars and the same-sex couples we see window shopping at the mall. Most often, it is our unspoken fears and misconceptions about others that keep us from truly opening our lives and sharing Christ's love. Through RoundTable Discussions, we hope to provide a venue for people to express their fears and beliefs in order to move beyond them and see people through God's eyes.

BLN RoundTable Discussions occur over a lunch period. Participants gather together, break bread and listen to the BLN team share and then open the floor to discussion in a safe environment. Participants are encouraged to feel safe sharing their questions and opinions, and to be respectful as they listen to others'. The value of these discussions is that people have a place to pose hard questions they have been afraid or have not had a venue to ask.

For example, in our post-9/11 world, many Americans have become fearful of Muslims. Though they know not all Muslims are terrorists, whenever they see a veiled woman or a Middle Eastern man, fear or anger grips their hearts. To address this issue, BLN has held several "Building Bridges to the Muslim Community" RoundTable Discussions. BLN invited guest speakers from the Muslim community to share what Muslims believe and what the average Muslim looks like in America. Participants were given the floor to ask questions and share their fears and misconceptions about Islam. Nothing can replace the education of actually meeting a person from the group we fear. We provide these opportunities and have witnessed many "aha" moments among those who attend.

Other BLN RoundTable Discussions have centered on the issue of interracial dating and marriage. Mixed-race couples have difficulty finding a home church, when each comes out of a unicultural church tradition. Outside of that, many people feel family pressure to marry within their own race or ethnicity, and feel torn when their choice of partner goes against their family's wishes. This is still a huge issue in the twenty-first century. The question arises, "How do I honor my father and mother in this?" The RoundTable Discussion has been a great way to hear people's hearts and hurts on this and many other topics.

A RoundTable Discussion is a great choice if your church, ministry or community has an elephant in the middle of the room that no one wants to mention. BLN does not shy away from any topic, no matter how potentially divisive or controversial. Our team is experienced with and equipped for asking the tough questions while maintaining an environment of openness and safety. The ultimate goal of these discussions is to bring people closer together through conversation as we lean on the Word of God.

TOWN HALL MEETINGS

While RoundTable Discussions usually occur over lunchtime with twenty to thirty participants, a Town Hall Meeting can have up to several hundred participants in attendance. This is a great venue for congregation- or communitywide discussions outside of a Sunday worship service. A typical Town Hall Meeting focuses on a single discussion topic, and BLN provides a keynote speaker or guest panel, which offers a variety of viewpoints. Dr. Anderson or another team member then opens the floor to discussion.

Before the 2008 presidential election, BLN held a Town Hall Meeting titled "Building a Bridge to the Ballot Box." The election was going to be historic, for many reasons. First, the economy had plummeted, people were losing jobs and their homes, and no one seemed to know how to fix it. Second, the wars in Iraq and Afghanistan seemed to have no end or exit strategy in sight, and many Americans were caught between supporting the troops and wanting an end to the wars. Third, the result of the election would give the United States its first female vice president or African American president. It was a high stakes election, to say the least.

For Christians in a multicultural congregation, there was another dimension to address: What if you valued diversity and truly wanted to see a person of color in the White House, but that candidate did not represent your personal political beliefs? How do you vote? Voices on TV, in the newspaper, on the Internet and radio clamored to give Christians the answer. BLN took another approach. Through this Town Hall Meeting, our goal was "to understand, not take a stand." We invited local and state politicians from both sides of the political debate to share where the two presidential candidates stood on a variety of issues. The audience asked questions that most mattered to their lives, and we all watched the final presidential debate together on a big screen at Bridgeway. In the end, Dr. Anderson encouraged each person to vote according to God's leading in their own life. Neither BLN nor Bridgeway Community Church endorsed a specific candidate or political party. We only endorsed active participation in the political process, suggesting individuals vote according to their consciences and pray for the new president, whomever it turned out to be.

This Town Hall Meeting brought together both church and community members from around Columbia, Maryland. If there is an issue that threatens the unity of your church or community and you would like to help bridge that divide through conversation, this format may be a good choice for you. Please keep in mind it takes at least three months of preparation time to arrange for panel speakers and other logistics for a Town Hall Meeting.

DETAILS

Our team is ready and equipped to serve you according to your ministry needs. If you did not see a service that fits your situation, we can customize a service for you. Keep in mind that BLN is a nonprofit organization with operating costs. Therefore there is a fee for all of our services, including those we create for you, with the exception of visiting a Bridgeway Sunday service.

YOUR TURN

I hope that after reading this book and reading about the variety of consulting services BLN offers, you have an idea of what your next steps will be. We have tried our best to give you practical advice and encouragement, knowing that if God has planted this vision in you, he has also equipped you with everything you need to accomplish it. As I said earlier, embarking on the journey of intentional multicultural ministry is not easy. Delving into the hard issues of racism, prejudice and class divisions in order to reveal those wounds to the light of the gospel is a commitment to loving the full body of Christ beyond our own comfort levels and trusting that God will bridge those divides for us.

One more thing. While challenging, multicultural ministry and crossing cultural lines can be a lot of fun! Visit Bridgeway once and you will see how the use of humor, dance, drama and other creative elements brings people together and manifests an atmosphere of joy. Only God can do this work. He takes the things of this world that divide, allows us to experience the discomfort (or pain) of working through those divisions and then allows us to glory in the joy of being united in him. We at Bridgeway pray that your ministry will be blessed to experience this joy and the fruit that comes with it on your journey of multicultural ministry.

Amy and Tim's Story

Amy and Tim have a culturally mixed family. Amy is Caucasian, Tim is African American, their oldest adopted son Matthew (4) is multiracial, and their newly adopted son Tyehu (18 months) was adopted from Ethiopia. They blend comfortably into the landscape of Bridgeway's multicultural congregation. That's one of the things Amy appreciates most about being part of the Bridgeway family. She admits, "It's refreshing not to be singled out and to be around people who look like us."

Amy and Tim began attending Bridgeway several years ago after they got engaged. They came from different church backgrounds and wanted to find a place where they both could feel connected and grow. As is the case with many interracial couples, the churches they visited were either predominantly white or predominantly black. According to Amy, while they did not feel totally uncomfortable in these unicultural churches, she recognized that at Bridgeway her "ability to worship freely was enhanced by feeling truly comfortable in the multicultural environment."

Finding a church that embraced and celebrated different cultures was especially significant for Amy. Since childhood, Amy had felt that God had planted a longing in her heart for diversity. Being surrounded by people at Bridgeway who "think and love like I do" provides her with a great sense of freedom and affirmation to be who God created her to be.

The multicultural environment has also been significant for Amy and Tim's extended family and children. "It's been great for our families to be able to come and worship and grow in our faith together. I don't think this could have happened in a non-multicultural church." For their children, the multicultural church family provides one of the best gifts of all. "I really believe that Matthew and Tyehu have been blessed with the opportunity to grow up seeing themselves as God sees them, not as the world sees them, because the two places they learn the most about God, home and church, reflect each other. For Matthew, a multiracial child, and Tyehu, a child born in a different country, it is a priceless gift to be affirmed for who they are, inside and out."

After six years, Amy and Tim have become so invested in the Bridgeway vision and mission that they both have joined the church staff. Tim serves as one of Bridgeway's technical directors, overseeing the video and media ministries of the church. Amy serves as the community relations assistant for Bridgeway's outreach ministries and also volunteers as the children's dance ministry leader. When asked for her final thoughts about what being part of an intentional multicultural church means to her, Amy said, "Bridgeway, to me, is a place that celebrates differences but does not exploit them. Everyone is 'different' in their own way, and that is exactly how God intended it to be. It is the only place in our lives where we, as a family, can rest in who we are."

CONTRIBUTORS

David A. Anderson is the founder and senior pastor of Bridge-way Community Church, a multicultural congregation in Columbia, Maryland. He is the founder and president of Bridge-Leader Network, a multicultural leadership consulting organization, and an instructor of cultural diversity at the University of Phoenix's Maryland campuses. Dr. Anderson received his bachelor's and master's degrees from Moody Bible Institute and his Doctor of Philosophy in the sociological integration of religion and society at Oxford Graduate School. His books include *Letters Across the Divide, Multicultural Ministry* and *Gracism*. A sought-after conference speaker, lecturer and consultant, he has had media exposure on over 2000 radio stations and television appearances, including Black Entertainment Television (BET), C-SPAN, TBN, PAX and ABC promoting his message of diversity. He also hosts a live radio show, *Afternoons with Dr. David Anderson: Your Bridge Building Voice in the Nation's Capital.* Dr. Anderson and his wife, Amber, reside in Ellicott City, Maryland, with their three children, Isaiah, Luke and Asia.

Rich Becker is executive director of creative arts ministry and cofounder of Bridgeway Community Church. His creative designs, desire for excellence, witty dramatic scripts, professional multimedia, uninhibited stage performances and team leadership have defined Bridgeway's artistic personality. Rich holds a bachelor's degree in marketing from the University of Illinois at Chicago. He is an active board member of the BridgeLeader Network and creative director for SharpStreet Creative. Rich, his wife, Beth, and their three children, Alex, Megan and Max, reside in Elkridge, Maryland.

Margarita R. Cabellon is the executive director of BridgeLeader Network. She coordinates trainings and speaking engagements on diversity issues with churches, businesses and other large organizations. She also creates educational opportunities for her local community to learn more about racial reconciliation and other diversity issues. Margarita is also the social networking coordinator of the *Afternoons with Dr. David Anderson* radio program. Margarita earned her B.A. in social welfare and M.S.W. from the University of Washington with a concentration in children, youth and families. Margarita was introduced to BLN when she and her husband, Paul, began attending Bridgeway Community Church in September 2004. Margarita and Paul welcomed their first son, Leo Emmanuel, into their lives in March 2009.

Frank V. Eastham Jr. is the principal of Oakland Mills High School in Howard County, Maryland. He obtained a bachelor's degree in education from West Virginia University and a master's degree in education from McDaniel College. He teaches leadership and diversity classes at Johns Hopkins University and McDaniel College. In April 2008, Frank was appointed as a commissioner for the Howard County Human Rights Commission. Frank has dedicated much of his life to the power of relationships and helping others build relationship skills. He has participated in and led mission trips to southern Sudan and Kenya, focusing on providing education for all children, leadership development and tribal reconciliation. Frank leads racial reconciliation seminars at Bridgeway Community Church and in his community.

Karen Eastham has been the director of BridgeKids, Bridgeway's children's ministries, since 1996. She earned her bachelor degree in elementary education from Towson University, where she received the Irene Steele Most Promising Teacher Award. Karen taught for seven years in the Howard County Public School System. Karen and her husband, Frank, live in Columbia, Maryland, with their three children, Sara, Will and Alli.

Nikki Lerner is a worship leader, speaker, performer and songwriter. Nikki has made it a priority to use her formal musical and vocal training along with her experience to encourage and equip the church. Nikki currently serves as the director of worship at Bridgeway Community Church. Nikki earned her Bachelor of Music degree from Towson University with a concentration in vocal performance and pedagogy.

Dave Michener is executive pastor of church ministries at Bridgeway Community Church, where he serves on the management team, giving leadership to the staff that serves BridgeKids, student ministries and adult church ministries. He also serves on the board of directors of the Association of Community Services of Howard County, a network for 140 nonprofit human resource organizations in Howard County, Maryland. Dave is a graduate of Baptist Bible College of Pennsylvania and has received his master of ministry degree from Moody Graduate School. He and his wife, Donna, reside in Columbia, Maryland, with their three sons, Davie, Dusty and Dakota.

Jared Sorber has served as pastor/director of student ministries at

Bridgeway Community Church since 2000. He earned his Bachelor of Religious Education from Davis College in 2000 and his Master of Arts in Ministry from Moody Bible Institute in 2008. Jared's experience in youth ministry includes serving at camps, city missions and local church and community-based nonprofit youth organizations. Jared is passionate about developing students and adult leaders into all that God has called them to be. Jared is a sports fan and loves to ski. In his free time Jared loves to spend time with his wife, Amie, and his sons Joel and Jake.

Dan Taylor has been part of Bridgeway Community Church since 1993, first as a volunteer and since 1996 as a pastor. The son of a pastor, Dan has always had a shepherd's heart for teaching and helping believers grow in their spiritual lives. He has a B.A. in pastoral studies from Moody Bible Institute and a master of ministry degree from Moody Graduate School. He has taught in multiple settings from summer camps to youth retreats, and served as an adjunct professor at Capital Bible Seminary. He and his wife, Lori, have one son, Steven.

Kwang Chul "KC" Whang is a commercial real estate broker and serves as a church elder at Bridgeway Community Church. He is also a board member of several religious, community and nonprofit organizations. He is a graduate of Middlebury College and has an M.B.A. from Rollins College Crummer Graduate School of Business. He and his wife, Dong, have three children, Grace, Peter and Faith.

ABOUT BRIDGEWAY COMMUNITY CHURCH

Located in Columbia, Maryland, Bridgeway is a nondenominational, multicultural church led by founding pastor and author on race relations, David Anderson. With over two thousand people attending each week, Bridgeway uses the creative arts and practical Christian teaching to reach people, no matter where they are on their spiritual journey.

The Command
Love God and love people
(Matthew 22—The Great Commandment;
Matthew 28—The Great Commission)

The Mission
To build into one another as we build bridges to our community

The Vision
To be a multicultural army of fully devoted followers of Christ moving forward in unity and love to reach our community, our culture and our world for Jesus Christ

The Values
B.R.I.D.G.E.S.

   Building into One Another
   Reconciliation—Spiritually, Racially and Relationally
   Instruction
   Dynamic Worship
   Growth—Personally and Spiritually
   Evangelism
   Service/Stewardship

The Strategy
Connect-Build-Equip-Lead

This strategy of progression in developing fully devoted followers of Christ is demonstrated in programs with the primary purposes of outreach, growth/inreach, ministry training and leadership development.

Connect. Helping people connect to Christ, our church and each other, *and* helping the church connect to the community

Build. Helping others grow in their walk as a fully devoted follower of Christ through the Word, worship, prayer, fellowship and sharing

Equip. Helping others grow in their walk as a fully devoted follower of Christ, and helping them see ministry to others as a natural outgrowth of that walk

Lead. Helping others grow in their walk, and helping them lead committed people (leaders who make other fully devoted Christ followers)

Bridgeway Community Church
9189 Red Branch Road
Columbia, MD 21045
Phone: 410-992-5832
Fax: 410-992-6761
E-mail: info@bridgewayonline.org
http://www.bridgewayonline.org

About BridgeLeader Network

BridgeLeader Network, Inc. (BLN), is a private, nonprofit 501(c)(3) organization whose mission is to assist, inspire and develop organizations to increase multicultural effectiveness.

BLN offers churches, businesses and corporations solutions to the problems of racial difference and offers proactive strategies to help them live the values of reconciliation and effective multiculturalism while making a profit. Today, BLN has ongoing relationships with Fortune 500 companies, accredited universities and other companies that desire to have a thriving and diverse workplace.

BridgeLeader Network, Inc.
9189 Red Branch Road
Columbia, Maryland 21045
Phone: 443-283-7219
Email: info@bridgeleader.com
http://bridgeleadernetwork.com/

About BridgeLeader Books

BridgeLeader Books are produced through a partnership between InterVarsity Press and BridgeLeader Network, a nonprofit organization that helps churches, colleges, companies and other groups move toward multicultural effectiveness. Addressing such topics as reconciliation, diversity and leadership development, Bridge-Leader Books contribute to a better understanding and practice of multiethnic ministry within the church and in the world.